Florida
Cow
Hunter

Bone was the subject of Frederic Remington's painting A Cracker Cowboy, *originally reproduced in the August 1895 issue of* Harper's New Monthly Magazine. *(Reproduction from the original black and white on canvas, 19 ½ x 23 ½ inches, in the collection of the "21" Club in New York City)*

Florida Cow Hunter

The Life and Times of Bone Mizell

Jim Bob Tinsley

University of Central Florida Press / Orlando

The University of Central Florida Press is a member of University Presses of Florida, the scholarly publishing agency of the State University System of Florida. Books are selected for publication by faculty editorial committees at each of Florida's nine public universities: Florida A&M University (Tallahassee), Florida Atlantic University (Boca Raton), Florida International University (Miami), Florida State University (Tallahassee), University of Central Florida (Orlando), University of Florida (Gainesville), University of North Florida (Jacksonville), University of South Florida (Tampa), University of West Florida (Pensacola).

Orders for books published by all member presses should be addressed to University Presses of Florida, 15 NW 15th St., Gainesville, FL 32611.

Copyright 1990 by the Board of Regents of the State of Florida
Printed in the U.S.A. on acid-free paper

10   09   08   07   06   05   P   11   10   9   8   7   6

Library of Congress Cataloging-in-Publication Data

Tinsley, Jim Bob.
Florida cow hunter: the life and times of Bone Mizell / Jim Bob Tinsley.
p. cm.
Includes bibliographical references.
ISBN 0-8130-0979-0.—ISBN 0-8130-0985-5 (pbk.)
1. Mizell, Bone, 1863–1921. 2. Cowboys—Florida—De Soto County—
Biography. 3. Cattle trade—Florida—De Soto County—History.
4. De Soto County (Fla.)—Social life and customs. I. Title.
F317.D4M598 1990   89-20609
975.9'5906'092—dc20   CIP

Dedicated to my wife, Dottie,
and to all of the Florida cowboys
we have known throughout the years

contents

preface

The cattle industry in the American West of the late 1880's was often troubled with frontier violence. During the same period, the open ranges of cow country in Florida were no different. The peninsular state had its own version of western lawlessness in DeSoto County and the surrounding ranges, where cattle wars, family feuds, rustling, assassinations, vigilantes, hangings, lynchings, cowtown duels, and fence-cuttings abounded. Into the thick of things rode Bone Mizell, an unlikely candidate for the most famous of the early Florida cowboys. Certainly he was the most colorful, the most quoted, and the most talked about.

A number of newspaper writers in Florida, including Donald McKay, Myrtle Hilliard Crow, and Wesley Stout, featured Bone Mizell and the cattle industry as their favorite topics on numerous occasions.

Donald Brenham McKay, born in Tampa in 1868, was founder, owner, and publisher of the *Tampa Daily Times* and served four terms as mayor of his hometown. From 1946 until his death in 1960 at age ninety-two, McKay edited and wrote a major portion of the popular "Pioneer Florida," a weekly page of vignettes in the *Tampa Tribune*. McKay knew Bone Mizell personally, and his early stories about the cowboy prompted readers who also had known him to send in additional tales. The last page by McKay appeared on September 11, 1960, three days after his death.

Myrtle Hilliard Crow's manuscript "Old Tales and Trails of Florida" was stored in a trunk in Kissimmee for nearly forty years before it was published for the first time in weekly installments between August 13, 1975, and September 23, 1976, in the *Osceola Sun*. The manuscript was completed in 1939 from personal interviews with Florida cow country pioneers.

Wesley Winans Stout, a former editor for the *Saturday Evening Post*, wrote a number of articles about Bone Mizell. Stout and his wife moved to Florida in 1949. He quickly acquired knowledge about Florida's past and started a historical column in 1952, called "The Beachcomber," which ran daily in the *Ft. Lauderdale News* for nineteen years. His last installment appeared on November 15, 1971, the day after his death in Louisville, Kentucky.

George H. Dacy wrote about Bone Mizell in his book, *Four Centuries of Florida Ranching*. South Florida brothers Albert and Park DeVane considered him a favorite topic, as did Miami writers Steven Trumbull and Nixon Smiley.

Locating illustrations for a book on Bone Mizell posed a problem, because very few photographs were taken in the cow country of Southwest Florida. Park DeVane of Sebring had four tintypes of Morgan Mizell family members in the 1880s made by an itinerant photographer. When the tintypes were reproduced here, they were printed in reverse to obtain the correct image.

I was able to track down two other important tintypes, owned by Margaret Smith of Dallas, Texas, one of David W. Mizell, the first sheriff of Orange County, Florida, and the other of his brother, Judge John R. Mizell. The Orange County Sheriff's Department had tried, unsuccessfully, to find a true likeness of David for their photo gallery of former sheriffs. Now they have one.

Following a visit to cowtown Arcadia, Frederic Remington, famed artist of the American West, chronicled the "Cracker Cowboys of Florida" in print and paint in the August 1895 issue of *Harper's New Monthly Magazine*. The subject of one of his six paintings was the illustrious cow-hunting raconteur Bone Mizell.

Back issues of *The Arcadian* were lost when a fire burned down the town of Arcadia in 1905, destroying valuable research material.

1

"The cracker wag of the Florida cow country"

"Kentucky had her Daniel Boone, Tennessee had her Davy Crockett, but Florida had her champion, 'Bone' Mizell, the pioneer cowboy humorist."

Morgan Bonaparte Mizell—Bone to most of his contemporaries—was a celebrity in Florida's cow country, a hard-drinking, fun-loving cow hunter who was the center of attention wherever he went. He was the subject of a painting by Frederic Remington in 1895 when the master artist of western scenes was in Florida. He made the front page of a metropolitan New York newspaper, and a ballad was written about one of his exploits. He worked with cows practically all of his life, first for his father, intermittently for cattle barons, and occasionally for himself. He never married, never owned a home, and seldom slept in a bed. The pine levels, palmetto scrub, and watery prairies of the vast Florida rangeland were his kingdom. "Ornery, tough and an incurable joker, Bone Mizell left his mark, however dubious, on the pages of Florida history. In time, he may prove to be Florida's best known, if not most typical cowboy."[1]

Bone's unconventional life-style and outlook were in many ways perfectly suited to the frontier environment in which he was raised and in which he worked all his life. Morgan Mizell,

Chief Billy Bowlegs, Indian leader of the Third Seminole War, which ended only six years before Bone was born. This photograph was taken in 1852. (Manatee County Historical Society)

Bone's father, moved with his half brother Enoch E. Mizell from Buddy's Lake community in old Hernando County to the sparsely populated Horse Creek (Chillockohatchee) settlement in Manatee County around 1862. Bone was born there in 1863, the eighth of twelve children born between 1850 and 1870 to Morgan Mizell and the former Mary Fletcher Tucker. When a post office was established, part of the Horse Creek settlement became Castalia. Later the town faded, and a nearby village was named Lily in honor of Lily Albritton, a distant cousin of Bone's.

During Bone's childhood, the country around Horse Creek, labeled "Rich Lands" on an 1842 Florida map, was mostly barren and unsettled and inhabited by wild animals. As late as 1853, Chief Billy Bowlegs still lived near Horse Creek on the west side of the Peace River, and the last of the Seminole Wars led by the colorful Indian leader had ended only six years before Bone was born. Wolves, bears, and wildcats were of great concern to early Horse Creek settlers because of stock predation. Even panthers, more often called "tigers" by early Floridians, were not uncommon in the region, and the remote flatlands were a haven for mosquitos, rattlesnakes, water moccasins, and alligators.

The first settlers along Horse Creek moved into the area during the Civil War without legal authorization and settled on land without title or right. Many of them had faced considerable prejudice because of their opposition to the "suicidal warfare" between the states.

In the winter of 1885–86, the Florida legislature authorized the selection of a new county seat for ten-year-old Manatee County to replace the one in the village of Manatee. Officials selected a site on Horse Creek in Township 37, conferring on it the name Pine Level. A rough log and clapboard courthouse, thirty feet by forty, was hastily constructed with puncheon floors and seats of similar materials. Ten years later, the nearest resident to the county courthouse was still a mile away. John Bartholf, the first postmaster in Pine Level, wrote about the homesteaders, "Although not owning a foot of land, they settled near the Court House and hewed from the land a rude log house and the necessary fencing material to enclose a few acres of land."[2]

It was not until 1883 that Bone Mizell's father owned the land on which he settled. On January 13, he bought between 86 and 87 acres in Township 35 for ninety cents per acre under the Internal Improvement Act of 1855, which entitled settlers to purchase swamp and overflowed lands of the state. Four years later, he acquired additional land under the same arrangement for one dollar per acre.[3]

Pine Level and Lily, only ten miles apart, became part of a new county when DeSoto was created out of Manatee in 1887. A year later, the two villages were bypassed by the railroad built down the east side of the Peace River, and the seat for the newly formed county was moved from Pine Level to a nearby village that had been named Arcadia for another Albritton girl. Lily became part of still another new county in 1921, when Hardee was formed out of DeSoto.

BONE was about six feet tall, rawboned and tanned to the color of a new saddle. He had sharp facial features, with a hawklike nose and protruding chin. For a number of reasons he looked old for his age. A daughter of Andrew J. McLenon, Mrs. Manila Coates, who ran the post office in Fort Ogden, remembers once when Bone came out of the woods after a prolonged stretch of cow hunting in bad weather and rode his horse into her front yard. He said he was tired of not getting any sleep, and, declining a bed, he lay down outside and went to sleep with a rock for a pillow.[4] A lifetime of this kind of exposure, combined with heavy drinking and a usually unkempt appearance, made Bone look older than he was. He talked with a lisping drawl and ended each sentence with an audible wheeze, characteristics he shared with his grandfather, Jesse Tucker.[5] Bone's boyhood companions laughed at his speech, and he developed a quick and cutting wit to overcome their barbs and mockery.[6] His life was a series of adventures and pranks, and although he was often the target of practical jokes himself, the last word was usually his. Former DeSoto County Sheriff J. L. (Les) Dishong recalled that "even the way he looked and talked made you laugh."[7]

Bone had only enough book learning to write his name. But although he could not read, write, or do sums, he carried in his head cattle accounts, brands, earmarks, and dewlap cuts for himself and his employers. He had a rare skill in the art of "mammying-up," the ability to match cows with their offspring at calving time; the number could often run into the hundreds for a single herd.[8] One pioneer, Mrs. Robert H. Roesch, the former Margaret Hunter, who lived in Pine Level when DeSoto County was created, said of him, "Bone was considered simple by many, but I declare he had more 'horse sense' than anyone I've ever known."[9] Another contemporary declared, "He could remember almost every cow or steer in a thousand head by their flesh marks."[10]

To recognize and remember individual ownership marks on Florida cattle took intelligence. A cowboy had to know his own personal marks, those of his employers, and those on thousands of range cattle belonging to a multitude of owners. A sample of complicated range heraldry is recorded in the description of a single herd that Bone bought from rancher Robert E. (Bob) Whidden in 1883. In addition to three different brands, earmarks in the herd were enumerated: "Upperslope, underbit in one ear, sharp in the other; Crop upper half crop split in one ear, sharp in the other; Upperbit in one ear, undersquare in the other; Undersquare in one ear, sharp in the other; Crop underslope split upperbit in one ear, sharp in the other; Crop, half crop split upperbit in one ear, undersquare in the other; Crop split underbit in one ear, under half flouar de luce [fleur-de-lis] in the other; Underslope split in one ear, uppersquare in other; Underslope split in one ear, crop upper half Crop in other, underslope, underbit, uppersquare."[11]

Bone was a foreman for Judge Ziba (Zibe) King, one of the largest cattle owners in the state, possibly the largest. He was said to own herds totaling 50,000 head and employed about ten men part of the time to care for cattle representing at least $400,000[12]—no job for a simple-minded cowboy.

Bone did conduct a somewhat successful mercantile business without assistance,[13] but his lack of education proved to be a handicap in running his Pine Level Grocery. Bookkeeping was too complicated, but he could make change if the customer paid cash. If the customer was broke, Bone would make a long black mark on the wall to indicate someone owed him something.

An amusing story is told about one of Bone's transactions. One Christmas morning "Aunt" Desdemony Driggers stopped by to wish the businessman a merry Christmas. Bone, in holiday spirits, told the aged pipe-smoking lady to look around the store and pick out a present for herself. She stopped at the tobacco shelf and inquired, "Do you mean I can pick just anything I

Morgan Bonaparte Mizell (1863–1921), known as Bone to most of his contemporaries. (Florida Photographic Achives, Tallahassee)

want, Bone?" "Sure thing, Desdemony," replied the genial merchant, "just whatever you see in this store that you want, I'm going to give it to you." "Well, then, Bone, I reckon you can just wrap me up a pound of that Toothpick terbaccy," decided Desdemony. "Ah, dog it, Desdemony," remonstrated Bone, "I mean to give you something fine and expensive, not just a pound of old terbaccy." Desdemony considered the offer as she puffed away on her cherished corncob pipe. Finally she drawled, "Well, if you feel that way about it, Bone, you can wrap me up about two pounds instead."[14] As the long black marks on the wall of the Pine Level Grocery began to crowd each other, the stock dwindled. When Bone found he could not remember who owed him for what, he closed up shop and went back to cow hunting.

Another story about Bone's lack of education is told by Logan King, a grandson of Ziba King. Once when Bone and a group of cowboys were driving a herd of cattle to Tampa for shipment, his old horse gave out. He saw an elderly black man plowing nearby and told the cowboys he was going to trade horses. Everyone told Bone he would have to give cash too because the plow horse looked better than his did. He rode over to the farmer anyway, and the cowboys saw Bone scribble on a piece of paper and then exchange horses. When Bone returned to the herd with his new mount, he was asked how he made the deal without any money. "Well, I give him a promissory note," Bone explained. "Why Bone, you can't read or write," said one of the cowboys. Bone smiled and replied, "Hell, he couldn't either."[15]

Never one for convention, Bone was what he was, with apologies to no one. Even without trying he was in trouble most of the time. He worried little about the future. His wardrobe consisted of what he had on—when he wore out a pair of boots, he bought another and left his old ones outside the general store.[16] He seldom dressed up, but on at least one occasion he outdid himself. Mrs. Robert Roesch said that the last time Bone visited her home in Pine Level, he was dressed in the finest clothing, including a pair of white spats. When she complimented the cowboy on his appearance, he responded, "I'm taking life easy now—instead of marking every fifth cow for my old boss, I'm marking them for Mr. Napoleon Bonaparte Mizell."[17]

Bone collected some cattle illegally during the turbulent 1890s in DeSoto County, when some cattlemen seemed to brand and claim everything in sight. He was arrested several times for rustling and for altering brands but was convicted only once. Honesty among cattlemen was never questioned, but ownership of cattle on the fenceless ranges continually caused trouble. Bone never seemed to worry about legalities. He simply got drunk instead.

When he was in his cups, he told his famous comical yarns—or became involved in another escapade that would itself become a popular tale. Many of his drunken exploits were true, but probably not all of them resulted from his own experiences. Although many stories have passed into oblivion, a number of them are still told today.

It was inevitable that drinking and a boisterous life would eventually silence Bone Mizell. Once he told a friend, "Some day when I'm about eighty-five or ninety they'll find me dead and everyone'll say, 'Well, old Bone's dead and liquor killed him.'"[18] He was right, except about the age. He died under the influence in Fort Ogden on July 14, 1921, at the age of fifty-eight.

2

"The Mizell family, prominent in the pioneer period in Florida"

"The word 'freedom' meant something special to the Mizells long before their names appeared on the muster rolls of George Washington."

The Mizell family made deep footprints in Florida's early history. Captain David Mizell, the first of the name in the territory, was born about 1770 in St. Matthew's Parish (now Effingham County), Georgia, the son of Charlton Mizell, a Revolutionary War veteran, and the former Elizabeth Everett.[1] David had three brothers, Charlton, Jr., Joshua, and John.

Around 1790, David Mizell moved to Camden County with his parents. He was commissioned a lieutenant in the Fifth Company of the county militia on May 9, 1801.[2] Following the death of his first wife, David moved back north to Bullock County, Georgia, where he was a captain of the militia in the Forty-ninth District from 1807 to 1809. He married Sarah Albritton in Bullock County on November 27, 1808. In 1813 and 1814, David was in South Georgia, serving as justice of the peace in the 381st District of Camden County. To help repel Indian attacks in 1817, he served in Major William Bailey's detachment of the Camden County militia.[3]

Exactly when David Mizell moved to Florida is uncertain, but census records for the territory show that in 1830 he and his wife lived in Alachua County near the Seminole Agency and Wanton's Post Office, later the community of Micanopy.[4] On June 28, 1833, David's brother John Mizell bought 500 acres in Alachua County from Thomas S. Clarke. The property was described as "Langs Hammoc, on the south side of Orange, Alias, Mizells Lake." The land was part of an 1818 grant to Clarke from the Spanish government and was described in Spanish as adjacent to "Laguna di Mizelles."[5]

A St. Augustine newspaper, under the dateline Newnansville, Florida, November 23, 1838, reported that Indians viciously attacked the family of John Tippins and his wife, Nancy, daughter of David Mizell: "Near the South Prong of St. Marys River, Tippins and his family, journeying from Georgia, were attacked by Indians. Tippins was shot twice and killed. Indians beat everyone else with tomahawks. Mother and infant daughter were killed. A three-year-old daughter was left for dead but survived."[6] According to one family historian, the attack took place east of the settlement known as Alligator, now Lake City, Florida. The family was on the way to David Mizell's home. The sole survivor, Cornelia Tippins, was chopped in the head with tomahawks and left for dead. From the safety of a nearby fort, witnesses to the horrible slaughter reported that the young girl was struck with tomahawks and then thrown into the air and impaled on the end of a spear as she came down.[7] But she lived eighty-five years longer.

David Mizell was a justice of the peace in Alachua County in 1848 and served as a county commissioner in 1849 and 1850.[8] On December 12, 1849, he purchased two tracts of land totaling 1,160 acres east of Newnans Lake in the same county.[9] He must have died soon after, for he is not listed in the Alachua County census for 1850.

Three sons of David Mizell and his first wife lived to raise families. Joshua, Joseph, and Enoch Everett Mizell were born in Camden County, Georgia. Another son of that marriage, Charlton, was born in the same county but died unmarried at the age of twenty-six. Two sons born to David Mizell and his second wife, Sarah, David, Jr., and Morgan, both raised large families.

Joseph Mizell and David Mizell, Jr., were still living with their families in Alachua County in 1850. Census records for that same year show that Joshua, Enoch, and their half brother Morgan were living with their families in Buddy's Lake community in Benton County, Florida.[10] Later that year, the name of the county was changed to Hernando.

On January 23, 1855, David Mizell, Jr., deeded his Alachua County property to his daughter Ann E. Roberts, wife of Albert Roberts. John Mizell's interest in land on Orange Lake was sold, along with two slaves and two horses, to Joshua Mizell on March 13, 1855.[11]

Morgan Mizell, Bone's father, volunteered for service in the war with Mexico on January 7, 1848, at Fort Brooke near Tampa. He was taken to Alachua County and placed in Company C, Florida Volunteer Battalion, under the command of Captain R. G. Livingston. Often called the Florida Independent Rifle Company, its effectiveness was reduced through sickness and death. Mizell became ill en route; he was sent to a hospital in New Orleans and from there to a hospital at Jefferson Barracks, Missouri, before returning home.[12]

The Mizell brothers were all active in the Seminole Indian wars. During the 1849 Indian troubles, Morgan was a third lieutenant in "Captain Mizell's Independent Company," commanded by his half brother Enoch.[13] These two brothers also took part in the Seminole War of 1856.[14]

On a clear, cool fall day in 1856, David Mizell, Jr., and his family as well as the family of his son, David William Mizell, left Alachua County in heavy wagons and headed farther south. According to David William's wife, the former Mary C. Pearce, the wagon train included riders on horseback and cattle, hogs, turkeys, and goats strung out for two miles along the trail. She recalls that as the caravan neared its destination, "the weather had got so hot, and we all thought it might be on account of our being so far South. It was dry, and there were flies and gnats, and the children would take turns getting out and walking in the deep, hot sand. I guess our water had spilled, or maybe we had given it to the team. Then, soon we were *all* walking, and thirsty, and leading the team. Then it started to rain. We camped, and had to cook in the rain. Next day, all day, it rained

Bone's father Morgan Mizell, seated between two unidentified Florida pioneers. (Tintype made around 1884; Park DeVane collection)

and the woods were full of water, and the awfullest deepest holes in the road, and the horses were falling down. Then everything stopped. Father said, 'This is it. We're here.'

"There was not one house! Poor Mother; we all gathered around her in the wagon trying to keep dry, and warm. It had turned cold then. She said, 'We haven't seen a house or a person for a week, so don't let yourselves get sick. There aren't any doctors, either.' Sister Sally was one year old that day. It was on Christmas Day, 1858."[15]

Upon the Mizells' arrival at their destination, one of the women in the party thrust a switch into the ground; it grew into a large sycamore tree that still marks the site. David, Jr., chose to build his home at a small settlement called Osceola on the In-

Bone Mizell around 1884; the women are believed to be his sisters. (Copied from an old tintype; Park DeVane collection)

Bone in his early twenties (right) and his brother Jess. (Tintype made around 1884; Park DeVane collection)

dian trail from Conway to Lake Jesup, overlooking the lake that now bears his name. His log cabin was the first erected in what became Winter Park. He was the first chairman of the Board of County Commissioners for Orange County and a member of the state legislature at the beginning of the Civil War.[16] Three of his sons, David William, John Randolph, and Thomas E., served with distinction in the war, and Thomas was killed in action.

Morgan Mizell, the youngest son of David, was the father of

Left to right: *Bone's father, Morgan, Bone, and Bone's uncle Enoch E. Mizell. (Tintype made around 1884; Park DeVane collection)*

six sons: Samuel P. (Sam), Bone, John Daniel, Ozian D. (Ocean), Silas (Si), and Jesse Bolivar (Jess). His daughters were Sarah Ann (Sally), Eliza McDonald (Mac), Mary Elizabeth, Cornelia Bradley, Margaret Carter (Peg), and Oregon Frances (Org). Four of them married: Sally to Madison W. Lewis, Mac to Owen Rufus Morey, Peg to Charles M. Johnson, and Org to William M. (Son) Albritton. Mary Elizabeth died at an early age, and Cornelia died from cancer as a teenager.

Jess, the only son to marry, wed the former Frances Michael Albritton. Elected sheriff of Manatee County in 1875, he served one four- year term and then went into the cattle business near Fort Thompson. According to his stepgranddaughter Dora McLenon Johnston, Jess was shot and killed during an argument on June 11, 1884.[17] (Other sources give the date of his death as June 13.) Sam Mizell grieved so much over the death of his brother that he had to be placed in the mental hospital in Chattahoochee, where he died and was buried. Ozian died in a Sarasota hospital after the death of his brother Bone. Little is known about Silas. Dora Johnston wrote in her memoirs that he was a telegraph operator, went to Alabama, and was never heard of again.[18] Bone became a major figure in the oral history of the Florida cattle industry.

3

"These killings are known as the Barber-Mizell feud"

"Some called it reconstruction, some called it a range war, while some others called it a feud. It may have been a little of all these factors."

When the steamer *Hattie* arrived downstream in Palatka in March 1870, it brought news to the populated parts of Florida that Sheriff David W. Mizell of Orange County had been waylaid and murdered while transacting official business in the cattle country deep in the upper reaches of the St. Johns River.[1] Within two months, the killing led to at least eight more related deaths in what came to be known as the Barber-Mizell feud.

The Barbers and Mizells had a "hereditary quarrel."[2] Both families migrated to South Georgia from North Carolina in the eighteenth century and later moved to the Territory of Florida.

Moses Edward Barber was born in Georgia in 1808. He arrived in newly established Columbia County, Florida, with his family in 1833, settling on the south prong of the St. Marys River a mile northwest of the present site of Macclenny. He built a stockade next to his log home for protection against Indians. It later became known as Barber Station, a stage stop on the route between Jacksonville and Tallahassee. Barber spent his time fighting Indians and rustling their cattle, driving the herds to

Barber's plantation on Big Creek near the St. Johns River, one of several homes owned by Moses E. Barber. This drawing was made while the farm was occupied by Union forces under Colonel William B. Barton just before the Confederate victory at nearby Olustee on February 20, 1864. (Harper's Weekly, March 12, 1864)

Georgia and beyond.[3] The Indians retaliated by killing one of his brothers.

Between 1850 and 1860, Moses' cattle interests ranged from the Carolinas to the upper St. Johns River marshes in South Florida. Research by a family historian supports the story that Barber had several homes and as many wives, all two-day cattle drives apart, between Augusta, Georgia, and central Florida. One of his part-time residences in a small community in Volusia County became Barberville.[4] But his fortunes were destined to wane.

Federal troops made Barber Station their headquarters prior to the Confederate victory at Olustee. Moses' wife, the former Maria Lea Alvarez, died, and his children grew up and left home. In March 1862, Moses married his twenty-three-year-old housekeeper, Rebecca E. Clements of Columbia County. Enemy soldiers reduced Barber Station to the home, a barn, three shanties, and two rail fences, and the eldest son of the patriarch was killed in a retreat in South Carolina just before the hostilities ended.

Moses headed south for a new start as a cattleman in Florida's postwar economy,[5] to Shake Rag, an Orange County settlement northeast of Lake Tohopekaliga. He consumed a large part of the cattle ranges before moving farther south to Canoe Creek Island, a large tract that actually became an island during high water.[6] Part of the Barber range included Ocean Prairie, a vast grazing area along the northern fringe of Jane Green Swamp. The legendary cattle baroness for whom the swamp was named is said to have been more than just an ally of Moses E. Barber.[7]

The Barbers directly involved in the bloody conflict with the Mizells were Moses Edward, his sons Moses B. F. and Isaac, and a nephew, Andrew Jackson (Jack) Barber, son of William W. Barber. Two of the participants had served in the Civil War, Jack in Roll Company H (Marion Hornets), Seventh Florida Infantry, in 1862–63 and Isaac in Roll Company I, Eighth Florida Infantry, in 1862. Isaac was later imprisoned at Fort Delaware.[8]

The main participants on the other side of the feud were brothers David William and John Randolph Mizell, Bone's first cousins. David W. Mizell was a private in the Seminole War for six months during 1857–58 in an independent company of the Florida Mounted Volunteers commanded by Captain Leroy G. Lesley.[9] In the Civil War he served as a corporal in Roll Company G, Eighth Florida Infantry.[10] On a march to Savannah, David was stricken with cholera and fell along the wayside while his company marched on. How he returned home is not known, but on his arrival he was told by a doctor that most of his insides were gone and that he probably would have to live on broth for the rest of his life.[11] John R. Mizell, a captain in Roll Company F, Seventh Florida Infantry, during the Civil War, was captured at Missionary Ridge near Chattanooga.[12] He was known as a "two-gun" man in later life, according to an Orange County historian who knew him: "It used to be said of him that when his opponent's eyes blinked, John pulled his gun."[13]

Military rule and martial law were introduced in Florida after the war, and civil government was not restored until July 4, 1868. Anxiety over emancipation, heavy indebtedness, the appointment rather than the election of public officials, and the emergence of and control by the Republican party were foremost in the minds of many Floridians. Reconstruction in Orange County brought about additional problems in the cattle industry. Because of lucrative Cuban markets and new settlers moving into the area, the value of beef increased rapidly, so much so that cattle were in greater demand than money. Rustling became so prevalent that honest cattlemen were forced to appropriate any stock they found to maintain their herds, and legalities had little meaning.[14]

The Barbers and Mizells were on opposite sides of the law.

David W. Mizell, Bone's cousin and first sheriff of Orange County, whose assassination on February 21, 1870, sparked at least eight more killings in the bloody Barber-Mizell feud. (Copied from a tintype; photo courtesy Margaret Smith)

*Downtown Orlando, county seat of Orange County, where the Bar-
ber- Mizell feud raged, taken before the turn of the century. (Photo
courtesy Florida Photographic Archives)*

"Despite the abundant cattle range, covering an area the size of
two present-day counties, there was not enough room for the two
families," one writer concluded.[15] The Barbers were not alone in
their bitter resistance to a postwar government that imposed
heavy taxes on their cattle herds, but they were among the most
aggressive. They were enraged when David W. Mizell was appointed sheriff of Orange County in 1868 by the Republican government and when his brother, John R., became judge of the
county civil and criminal courts. Following an incident in which
Sheriff Mizell drove off some Barber cattle for nonpayment of
taxes, Moses E. Barber issued a personal threat to the sheriff to
stay off Barber property or he would leave "feet first."[16]

The fall term of the Circuit Court of Orange County was
scheduled to open in the log courthouse on Monday, October 26,
1868. A newspaper correspondent, covering court proceedings
in Volusia County the week before, commented on the setting for
the upcoming court week in Orlando: "I would like to say something of this beautiful country, of its charming lakes and
magnificent orange groves, but cannot now."[17] But a number of
things were neither charming nor "magnificent" in Orlando.
Sometime over the weekend, one or more persons set fire to the
courthouse, and despite the efforts of bucket brigades from the
town well, manned by men in their nightclothes, the log struc-

ture burned to the ground, destroying practically all county records. A temporary courtroom was hastily set up next door in a hotel, and the circuit court was opened on schedule by Sheriff Mizell with Judge John W. Price presiding. Armed cattlemen and cowboys stood around the makeshift courtroom during cattle cases and glared at the public officials. Not one of them would testify against another.[18]

The first case was against a cowboy charged with illegally altering the mark of an animal. The defendant failed to appear, and the court ordered that securities be called and recognizance be forfeited. Later in the day, four different bills were presented against Moses B. F. Barber for arson, adultery, forcibly confining and imprisoning another against his will, and maliciously threatening an injury to the person and property of another with intent to compel a person to do an act against his will. On the third day of court, a true bill was returned against Moses E. Barber, Moses B. F. Barber, and Thomas Johnson, charging that on August 18, 1868, they forcibly confined and imprisoned George Bass of Orange County against his will. The case was continued and bail fixed at $500 for Moses B. F. Barber with capiases issued for the others.[19]

Lawlessness in Orange County was the major consideration of the grand jury with the opening of the court's spring term the following year. In its presentment, signed by foreman David Mizell, father of the sheriff, the grand jury commented: "We regret the evident spirit in some parts of the County to take the Law into their own hands, but having confidence in the Courts, they [the Grand Jury] believe that by the rigid enforcement of the Laws the evil has been checked." The investigative body also went on record to say they regretted the burning of the courthouse and urged all citizens to unite in an effort to reestablish the county's records. They asked all citizens to thank their efficient clerk, A. H. Stockton, for the caution he exercised in preserving many important papers connected with the courts of Orange County.[20]

On May 1, 1869, Moses E. Barber was found guilty of polygamy and ordered to pay a $500 fine and stand committed until paid.[21] A separate indictment on the same day charged that on August 19, 1868, Moses E. Barber and Moses B. F. Barber confined and imprisoned William Smith of Orange County against his will with force and arms.[22] In the pending case of the earlier charge involving George Bass, the three defendants failed to appear and trial was rescheduled for a special term in July.[23] Moses E. Barber appeared in court as a defendant in the case on July 22, 1869, and entered a plea of not guilty. Cases were continued against his codefendants, who again did not appear.[24]

During the trial, George Bass charged that Moses E. Barber was one of three parties who unlawfully took him prisoner while he was driving cattle in south Orange County on August 18, 1886. He testified that the heavily armed men took his horse by the bridle and led him off, threatening and detaining him for a half-hour. He claimed that Barber informed him, "George, we have three propositions to make. Leave the County in thirty days or take one hundred lashes or have your neck broke." In a final accusation, Bass told the jury, "I recognize Moses E. Barber, prisoner at the bar, as one of the party."[25]

Having no witnesses to introduce in his behalf, Barber asked leave of the court to make a statement and his request was granted. He claimed that after he came upon Bass in the woods, he noticed that part of the herd did not belong to the plaintiff. "I rode round the cattle and looked at them," he testified. "Three of the steers belonged to cattle I had formerly owned, two of them the Stock A. J. and the other B. flower de lu [fleur-de-lis], and the other of Johnsons Stock." Barber informed the court that Bass asked for ten days in which to leave the county, and Barber told him he could have twenty or thirty. "As to my arresting him or any thing of that sort, I did not," Barber continued. "I neither put my hand upon him nor attempted to prevent his going where he pleased. I gave him the best advice I was capable of doing, and he agreed to it and we settled it."[26]

On July 22, 1869, the jury found Moses E. Barber guilty as charged and recommended him to the mercy of the court. Two days later, he was sentenced to the state penitentiary in Leon County for one year.[27]

Sheriff David W. Mizell of Orange County had been called upon for evidence in the case after the counsel for defense claimed the incident happened across the line in Brevard County. He testified that people in the area transacted their busi-

Andrew Jackson (Jack) Barber with his second wife, Annie Hull Jack-son in 1896. Jack's role in the Barber-Mizell feud ended when he was tried for cattle larceny and sentenced to the state penitentiary; he later became a prominent cattleman and owner of a fine citrus grove. (Photo courtesy Robert W. Barber)

ness in Orlando, so their residence was recognized as a part of Orange County.[28]

Barber tradition maintained that numbers of Barber cattle had been stolen but that Sheriff Mizell had not attempted to stop the lawlessness. A prize heifer belonging to Jack Barber is said to have been found in the Mizell herd with an altered brand. Jack reclaimed his property, but when the sheriff caught him he had butchered the animal. Although he could account for the hide, the Barber brand was said to have been completely obliterated. Jack was tried for cattle larceny and sentenced to the state prison. Sheriff Mizell escorted the prisoner down the St. Johns River to Palatka, from where he was to be transported overland by stage to the penitentiary. Moses E. Barber insisted on going along with his nephew to protect him from "foul play." While on the boat to Palatka, Jack Barber asked the sheriff for his chewing tobacco. Mizell responded by shoving the plug into the mouth of the prisoner, cutting his lip. Angered by the incident, Moses told the officer in no uncertain terms, "This day, Dave Mizell, you've started on the road to Hell!"[29]

Robert Bullock, an Orange County cattleman, held a bill of sale on a number of cattle but had not been successful in getting payment. Sheriff Mizell headed south into the vast Barber ranges to collect the debt or return the cattle to Bullock.[30] Accompanying the sheriff were his brother Morgan M. Mizell, an Orange County justice of the peace from 1863 to 1865, and William Mizell, the sheriff's twelve-year-old son.

On February 21, 1870, the party was crossing Bull Creek south of Deer Park when the stillness was shattered by a single gunshot. Sheriff Mizell toppled from the saddle, mortally wounded. In an attempt to make the Mizell youth think that Indians had killed his father, the killer gave a loud war whoop. William and his uncle dragged the dying sheriff onto a tussock, and the older Mizell set out for help, leaving young William to guard his father. Morgan soon met up with George Sullivan, who then hastened to Bull Creek Ford to stay with William. The son later recalled that his father died praying for his enemies and asked that no one seek revenge against his killers.[31]

But the aftermath of the assassination was bloody. Official records do not tell the story, and at the time people were hesitant to discuss the matter. A former sheriff of Osceola County, Young

Tindall, heard the story from his father, who was twenty years old when the conflict occurred. "For many years it wasn't safe to be a friend of either side—unless you kept your mouth shut," Tindall confided.[32]

When word of the murder reached Judge John R. Mizell in Whittier, a settlement east of Kenansville that no longer exists, he was not misled by the Indian cry of the assassins. Only one person, in his mind, was responsible for the shooting of his brother. He gathered a posse headed by newly appointed Sheriff Jack Evans and went after Moses E. Barber and his confederates. Upon hearing that Needham (Needs) Yates, a Barber employee, was present when the sheriff was slain and might have actually been the trigger man, the posse scoured the countryside until it located him in a scrub a few miles northwest of Kissimmee. The story is that Yates was stood upon a pine stump and riddled with bullets and buckshot. Needs Scrub got its name as a result of the gruesome encounter.[33] A Tampa newspaper, the *Florida Peninsular,* reported at that time that Needham Yates and John Yates were arrested and killed in an escape attempt.[34]

Moses and one or more Barbers headed north when they heard that riders were after them. They were almost overtaken at a creek ten miles southeast of Orlando, but the posse's horses bogged down in the marshes of a stream that has since been called Boggy Creek, and Moses and his kinsmen got away. Undaunted, the avengers sought other Barbers. The younger Moses Barber was captured at Lake Conway near Orlando. The posse rowed the unfortunate captive out on the lake, weighed him down with a heavy plowshare around his neck, and rolled him overboard. When it appeared that Barber would make it to shore in spite of his burden, the posse opened fire and killed him. Isaac Barber was captured, taken to the home of Sheriff Evans, and reportedly killed when he attempted an escape. His grave marker near Kissimmee gives the date of his death as March 20, 1870. Moses E. Barber and Jack Barber were nowhere to be found.

The strife-torn scene of the vendetta covered portions of southern Orange County and a part of southwestern Brevard County, with the determined posse either heedless of judicial limits or unsure of county lines. Exactly how many persons were killed in the Barber-Mizell feud is not known. The sole authorita-

Artist's drawing of the slaying of young Moses Barber at Lake Conway. (Bob Lammb, Sunday Magazine, Miami Herald, *April 16, 1967)*

tive count, covering only the first half of the year, is found in the mortality schedules of the 1870 U.S. Census for Orange and Brevard counties, and it appears to be incomplete. The lists name seven men killed in the conflict, but as the enumerations covered only a limited time of the bitter struggle, they probably do not represent the real total. With the addition of two other victims whose deaths were published in a Tampa newspaper during the conflict, the known killings recorded at the time are at least nine men in less than three months.

Part of the bloody arena for the killings was in the disputed no-man's-land along the ill-defined boundary between Orange and Brevard counties, causing the names of two victims (Isaac Barber and Needham Yates) to be recorded on both county lists. For the period January 1–June 1, 1870, the census taker for Brevard County lists three participants shot and killed in the bloodshed: Isaac Barber, age thirty-two, Needham Yates, age fifty-three, and Lyell Pagett, age thirty-six. On the Orange County list for the same months are six men involved in the conflict. David Mizell, forty-year-old sheriff of the county, is listed as a fatal gunshot victim, as are Isaac Barber and Needham Yates. The other three are William Yates, age fifty-two, and William Bronson, age twenty-eight, listed as having died of gunshot wounds, and Moses Barber, age thirty-seven, entered as a drowning casualty. Moses E. Barber, however, is not listed on the mortality schedule of either county. All of the gunshot victims enumerated on the Orange County list, with the exception of Sheriff Mizell, have an "X" before their names. Further comment on the related deaths is entered by the enumerator at the bottom of the page: "David Mizell, Sheriff, was waylaid and murdered by Parties Unknown. All the others where Gunshot wounds are given as Cause of Death were Arrested by Deputy Sheriff upon suspicion of being instrumental in the death of Mizell and shot while attempting to escape."[35]

On April 13, 1870, the *Florida Peninsular* again called attention to the horrible outrages in Orange County and began to question the so-called escape attempts of the slain prisoners. The newspaper condemned Sheriff Jack Evans as a "tool of the Radicals," recalling that he was well known in Tampa "and had to leave here with a load of buck-shot in his back for his general rascality."[36] The same newspaper incorrectly reported the following month that "Old Mose Barber was waylaid and murdered on the 10th inst." and decried continuation of the war with no call for troops to stop the outrages and no declaration of martial law from Harrison Reed, the unpopular Massachusetts-born governor of Florida.[37]

In a meeting on January 14, 1871, the clerk of the Orange County Commission presented accounts of David W. Mizell, late sheriff of the county, in the amount of $136.36 for services performed in criminal suits disposed of during the October 1870 term of the circuit court. In addition, the clerk was ordered to issue a warrant for $70.30 for services of the sheriff in preparing tax books, copying books, making out and copying additional tax lists, and making out, copying, and certifying previous tax assessments for 1867, 1868, and 1869. The document was signed by David Mizell, chairman of the Board of County Commissioners for Orange County and father of the late sheriff.[38]

An official indictment against Moses E. Barber for the murder of Sheriff David W. Mizell was not filed until November 11, 1870.[39] In the meantime, Moses had disappeared. Despite the press report of his murder, a family descendant and researcher says that Moses and his nephew Jack Barber escaped northward by boat on the St. Johns River, then headed west, and were later traced to Wakulla County.[40]

Moses is said to have ridden to North Florida and stopped at

The log home of David W. Mizell, built by his wife Angeline on the shores of Lake Rowena and photographed in 1888. Left to right; Angeline A. Mizell; Jessie Mizell, wife of Bone's uncle Thomas Mizell; Thomas Mizell; and Duncan C. Pell, who bought the old home. The children are Lula May Arnold and Mary Lee Mizell. (Orange County Historical Museum)

some of the Barber "widows" to tell them that if they wanted their cattle and land in the Kissimmee area they could go and claim them; he wanted no part of that country again.[41] Columbia County records indicate that Moses E. Barber died intestate on November 27, 1870. His legal widow, Rebecca E. Barber, petitioned for a letter of administration one month later.[42] Financial troubles mounted against Barber in North Florida. In 1870 a Duval County lawsuit charged him and an associate for nonpayment of a $111,166 mortgage. Foreclosure proceedings were completed on Christmas Eve of the same year, but by then the controversial cattleman was dead.[43] Rebecca was named administratrix in a receivership case in Orange County against the estate of the deceased that listed cattle sales and vouchers for amounts paid to numerous individuals during 1871–72.[44]

Andrew Jackson Barber, Moses' nephew, had been an Indian fighter before serving in the Confederate Army. He later became a cattleman and raised from seed one of the finest citrus groves

Judge John R. Mizell, Bone's cousin and a leading Florida Republican during Reconstruction. (Copied from an old tintype; photo courtesy Margaret Smith)

in a part of Orange County that later became Osceola County.[45] The last surviving Barber participant in the infamous cattle feud, Andrew, died at his home in the Conway section of Orange County on August 18, 1916, a widely known and respected pioneer.[46]

William David Mizell, who witnessed the assassination of his father at Bull Creek, was born in a covered wagon en route to Orange County in 1858. He died in 1883 at the age of twenty-five.

Judge John R. Mizell was a colorful figure in Florida history for many years after the feud. He settled on the shores of Lake Mizell near Orlando, where he owned a fine orange grove. His neighbor, Thomas Charles Bridges, described an incident involving the rugged landowner. Some waiters at the Seminole Hotel in 1894 had been stealing oranges from the Mizell grove. When the judge saw the thieves load a sack of oranges into a boat and row off, he called to them to return to shore. They not only refused but began to ridicule him from the boat. According to Bridges, "Mazell's [sic] fist went to his hip and came back grasping a heavy .44. The sharp reports cracked like a whip-lash across the lake, and, as the big bullets crashed one after another into the stern of the boat, exactly on waterline, the terrified waiters yelled for mercy. The judge kept on until he had emptied his pistol, and by that time the boat was so badly holed that it was sinking. The wretched waiters swam ashore and stood dripping in the shallow water, afraid to come farther." Before letting the culprits go, Mizell told them he figured it would have been cheaper for them to come back when he first called them.[47]

In later years, Judge Mizell moved to the lower east coast of Florida and once again became involved in government services. On June 6, 1908, the town of Pompano was incorporated and its first municipal election was held. Judge Mizell was chosen the first mayor of the town, and G. R. Snell was elected marshal.[48]

Once the leading Republican politician in the state of Florida, the judge retired from many years of public service in 1910 to live on his farm near Pompano. He died on November 9, 1913, in Miami while visiting his daughter Mary A. King,[49] wife of harness maker William C. King.

4

"A cowboy's cowboy"

"Bone Mizell was just a typical cowboy—the way Paul Bunyan was a typical lumberjack."

Bone Mizell grew up as a cowboy, as did most of the young men around him. In the late 1800s, the cattle industry was a way of life for those born in the interior section of southwest Florida. According to one writer of the era, "The natives are brought up to the business from youth, know little else, and like nothing better than to be given a horse and dog and the care of a herd."[1]

As a young man, Bone helped his father in the family's cattle business. On January 3, 1887, he bought 1,000 head of cattle ranging in Manatee and Monroe counties from Nathan C. Platt for $6,000. At the same time, Bone, his father, his brother John, and his sister Mary sold Platt 500 head of their cattle for $3,000.[2] On February 25, 1887, the *Fort Ogden News* reported that Bone had purchased the cattle stock of F. M. Platt.[3] When his father died, Bone took over the family's cattle operation. He was shrewd in his dealings and knowledgeable about cattle, but heavy drinking, wild sprees, and generosity toward his friends soon took everything his father left him. The explanation in his own simple philosophy was "Them that's got, has got to lose. Them that hasn't, kaint."[4]

Bone was a rover by nature. For him, the open ranges were home, although he did own some property as a young man. On January 8, 1885, he bought forty acres of land near Pine Level from John W. Johnson and Mary Johnson for $415. A year later, Bone and his first cousin Joseph Mizell paid Barbara E. Thomas and James M. Thomas $180 for thirty acres near Lily.[5] Bone purchased two lots in Sibley's Central Division in the town of Charlotte Harbor on January 13, 1889, but he soon sold the property. On June 17, 1889, Martha Youmans bought one parcel for $64. Two years later, the bachelor cowboy sold the other lot to Charles G. Breniza for $50.[6]

Shortly thereafter, Bone was back in the stock business for himself. Between 1891 and 1895, he registered sixteen personal cattle brands and nine hog marks in DeSoto County.[7] In the spring of 1892, Bone bought a stock of cattle from his friend Bascomb Smoot (Back) Johnson. Later that year, he sold the herd to cattleman Bob Whidden for $1,150. During the summer, Bone also purchased stock from Howell T. Lykes, founder of the Lykes shipping and cattle empire. This herd, known as the Lykes stock cattle, ranged south and east of the Peace River and north of the Caloosahatchee River. In 1893 Bone paid Bob Whidden $1,400 for cattle ranging in DeSoto and Lee counties.[8]

But Bone's success as a cattle owner was short-lived. He was a free-spending cowboy, and his career in high finances came to a close in a fashion that typified his gregarious generosity. After a deal in which he received $1,000 for some fine cattle, Bone decided to throw a party for his friends. One version of the story claims Bone spent $9,000 for the party, money he supposedly received as payment for a herd of Spade branded cattle belonging to Judge Ziba King.[9] Another version says Bone chartered a steamer in Tampa, and without knowing or asking what the cost would be, he and his friends cruised for several days with food and drink served at Bone's expense.[10]

P. R. Reed owned the Bar and Grill in Arcadia. He recalled that Bone chartered a boat for his friends and they went down the Caloosahatchee and into the Gulf of Mexico, where the rudder

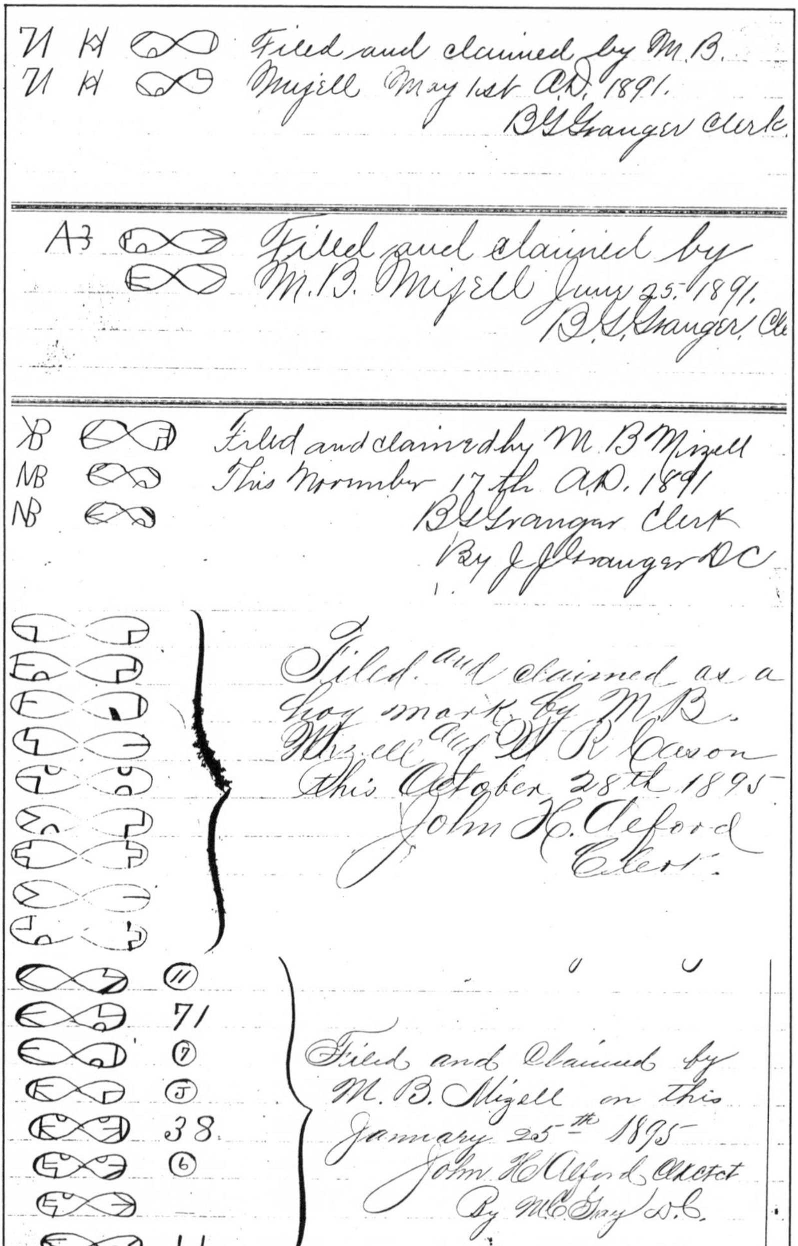

71 Η ∞ Filed and claimed by M. B.
71 Η ∞ Mizell May 1st A.D. 1891.
B.G. Granger Clerk

A3 ∞ Filed and claimed by
∞ M. B. Mizell Juny 25. 1891.
B.G. Granger, Cle.

XB ∞ Filed and claimed by M. B Mizell
NB ∞ This November 17th A.D. 1891
NB ∞ B.G. Granger Clerk
By J.G. Granger D.C.

Filed and claimed as a
hog mark by M B.
Mizell and W R Carson
this October 28th 1895
John H. Deford
Clerk.

11
71
7
J
38
6
1 L.

Filed and Claimed by
M. B. Mizell on this
January 25th 1895
John H. Alford Clerk
By M.C. Gay D.C.

RO or Filed and claimed by

Cattle brands and hog marks registered by Bone Mizell. (From Marks and Brands I, DeSoto County, Clerk of Circuit Court Office, Arcadia, Florida, pp. 11, 12, 15, 21, 50, and 58) broke and the boat drifted into a heavy wind. According to Reed, the jolly cowboy climbed up on the cabin with a bottle of booze and broke into song:

Fare ye well Miss Mary Ann,
Fare ye well I say,
The rudder's broke and the winds blow strong,
O fare ye well today.[11]

Probably the most reliable firsthand details of the escapade were told by Bone's friend Bob Whidden, with whom he had numerous cattle dealings. According to Whidden, Bone chartered a steamer operated by Captain Clay Johnson and invited his cowboy buddies to cruise the Kissimmee River with him. He had them served with all the food and champagne they could drink, which was plenty. When they returned, Bone was asked if he regretted spending all his money and having nothing left to show for it. He replied that he was satisfied with being "powerful rich" for one day, and showing his friends a fine time was exactly what he wanted to do. Whidden added that Bone "went back to cow hunting again and was very happy."[12]

It was as a cowboy, not as a businessman, that Bone achieved his place in Florida folklore. The more familiar cowboy of the western plains and mountains had nothing on this cow hunter of the Florida scrublands, who was described by a contemporary as "an expert horseman and a crack shot with rifle and sixgun, lightning fast at roping and branding, and no four-legged brute too big or too bad for him to tackle and master."[13] Even discounting this possible exaggeration, Bone was known as a topnotch cowboy, and at different times he was employed by three of Florida's most famous early cattle ranchers.

Judge Ziba King was almost as celebrated as his foreman Bone. A native of Homerville, Georgia, King became a Florida beef baron and a Fort Ogden merchant, was a member of the state legislature, took part in the DeSoto County range wars, and owned his own bank; a historical park was named in his honor after his death. King is believed to have left instructions to his sons that after he died, they were to pay Bone $500 a year, provide him with a good horse, and keep—or

Far right: *Pioneer cattleman and citrus grower Robert Early (Bob) Whidden, photographed in 1910. Left to right: the wife of Whidden's grove foreman, Whidden's daughter Ruby Elaine, Mrs. Robert E. Whidden, and grove foreman (name unknown). (Photo courtesy Barbara Welles Probasco)*

get—him out of jail when needed.[14] This must have been a verbal understanding, for the request is not verified in King's will.[15]

King's cattle ranges joined the vast holdings of the Parkers, another outfit for which Bone worked. The Parkers shared with King a part of the open rangeland known as Ninety Mile Prairie, extending from the Kissimmee River to the Gulf of Mexico. Headquarters for the family enterprise, which belonged to Lewis, Thomas, and J. Newton Parker, was on the frontier near Joshua Creek. The three brothers were sons of Captain John Parker, a veteran of the Seminole Wars, an officer in the Confederate army, and a prominent pioneer cattleman himself.

Newton Parker was the father of Zeb, Smiley, Aussie, Accum, and Hooker Parker, who organized the third-gener-

Judge Ziba (Zibe) King, DeSoto County cattle baron. (Florida Photographic Archives, Tallahassee)

ation Parker cattle operation in the early 1900s. Just before World War I, the Parker brothers merged with the sons of Ziba King—T. B. (Buck), H. L. (Dick), Garfield (Bet), John (Bull), Russell, and Eugene—to form the King-Parker cattle dynasty. Bone Mizell tended cattle for all of them.

He also worked for Colonel Eli O. Morgan. In the late 1800s, Morgan sold his ten-room hotel in Pine Level, bought

Jasper Newton Parker, who with his brothers and sons ran the Parker cattle empire in DeSoto County. Parker died in 1896 at the age of forty-five. (Photo courtesy June Parker Whidden)

additional stock, and moved to Fort Basinger on the Kissimmee River to set up a large cattle operation. He became one of the most prominent and respected cattleman in southern Florida.

The cattle country Bone worked covered nearly all of the Florida peninsula from Orlando south to the upper Everglades. For thirty-four years of his life, DeSoto County consisted of 3,750 square miles, extending from Charlotte Harbor on the west coast to Lake Okeechobee and the Kissimmee River on the east. In 1921, the year Bone died, his home

A Parker cowboy prepares food on the open range. (Photo courtesy June Parker Whidden)

county was subdivided into Hardee, Charlotte, Highlands, and Glade counties. The vast prairies, stretching undisturbed in all directions, appeared ideal for stock raising. A resident of Pine Level wrote in 1876 about the advantages these open ranges had over those in other states: "The idea of a man's toiling from early dawn to late at night five months in the year to feed himself and stock the remaining seven seems to be so absurd to us, who never need to feed our stock at all, as it keeps in good order all the year round, and who farm at all seasons, keeping up a continual succession of crops, all more or less productive and profitable."[16]

One disadvantage was ever present, however. During the rainy season, streams continually overflowed their banks, and cattle paths had yet to be worn from one depression to another. The flatlands were a veritable sea of water with the excess escaping only by seepage and evaporation. This condition and its corresponding humidity caused a prevailing weather that was most disagreeable.[17] Moreover, the open ranges in the southern part of Florida were deficient in essential minerals, and the grass had little nutritional value. Twenty or more acres were needed to support one cow.

The cattle tended by Bone and his contemporaries represented greatly deteriorated stock from that introduced by Ponce de León and other Spanish explorers. By the time the Spanish withdrew from Florida in the early 1700s, they had built up a substantial cattle industry. Remnants of their cattle crossed with the poor-quality stock owned by early English settlers, evolving into a distinctive type well adapted to Florida range conditions. The hardy animal rarely weighed over 600 pounds.[18]

In Bone's time, the foundation stock in Florida was called the native cow, scrub cow, and occasionally the less flattering

Florida scrub cattle purchased by the King brothers and placed in a corral prior to branding and assigning to other herds. This photograph was taken at the Kings' citrus grove headquarters four miles south of Arcadia. The one-armed man in front of the fence on the left is Bet King; beside him is Buck King. (Photo courtesy H. Logan King, Jr.)

"knot head." Due to the rawboned, undernourished condition of the small animals, they were known to some as "4-H cattle: hide, hair, hoofs, and horns."[19] The stock deteriorated further when some owners exported their better males to Cuba for bull fighting.[20]

When butchered, the beef was just as tough on the table as it was on the hoof. While staying at his summer home and laboratory in Fort Myers in 1887, Thomas Edison compared the meat to belting, and it was generally agreed that persistent hacking was required "to cut and divide the gravy."[21] A fringe benefit of the food was humorously expressed by a young soldier in 1898 while awaiting his ship to Cuba during the Spanish-American War. In a letter to his mother, the soldier wrote that if he ate much more Florida beef he would be bulletproof.[22] In fact, the quality of Florida cattle remained low until the mid-1900s when the state was declared free of cattle ticks, the open range declined, and ranchers began to use purebred stock to upgrade their herds.[23]

The Florida cowboy worked under extremely harsh conditions that included tormenting insects, wild animals, oppressive heat, and torrential rains. The major ranchers in DeSoto

A fine Florida longhorn, owned by early Arcadia rancher Ed Welles. (Photo courtesy Claude C. Jones, Jr.)

Parker cowboys pose near their ox-drawn supply wagon in a cow camp on the vast ranges of Ninety Mile Prairie. (Photo courtesy June Parker Whidden)

County owned from 5,000 to 10,000 head of cattle, with a few owners tallying 12,000 to 30,000 head. Individual cowboys were typically put in charge of 100 to 500 head each, making it easier for them to recognize their cattle if they mixed with another herd. Frequently the cowboys helped each other by riding together and tending to their many separate herds as a group. For his services the cowboy received an average of one dollar per day and board.[24] Some DeSoto County cattlemen gave individual workers two beeves a year and every fifth calf.[25] This gesture enabled cowboys to build up sizable herds for themselves over the years.

The palmetto cowboys lacked the glamour often associated with their Western counterparts. Their dress, for example, was hardly spectacular. Many wore cheap, wide-brimmed wool hats that cost seventy-five cents to a dollar each. When the hats became full of dirt and grease, they were wind resistant and waterproof. Instead of slickers, Florida cowboys wore ponchos made of a four-by-six piece of wool or cotton blanket, gutta-percha, or oilcloth. Boots worn by many of the cowboys were manufactured in Boston. The tops extended above the knees for protection from saw grass and snakes. Some cowboys wore brogans, shoes common to most backwoodsmen. Hickory shirts and heavy cotton pants completed their attire. Frontier artist Frederic Remington was disappointed in the Florida cowboy's bedraggled appearance. He gave this description of two cowboys that rode by him in Arcadia: "They had on about four dollars' worth of clothes between them, and rode McClellan saddles, with saddle bags, and guns tied on before."[26] The old military saddles had an opening down the seat, affording ventilation for horse and rider and making them cooler than western rigs in the humid Florida climate. Saddle horns were not an absolute requirement because ropes were less useful in the dense underbrush than the preferred cow lashes. Those who brandished the long, menacing whips became known as the "cracker cowboys."

One year after Remington's characterization of the Florida cowboy was published, a Jacksonville newspaper correspondent gave a description of a cattleman from the same area. The cowboy rode a small, sorry-looking Texas pony. His rig consisted of a saddle with a much-worn "Texas tree," rope girth and stirrup straps, and a rope bridle with heavy curb bits. Suspended from the pommel was a regulation cow whip; a ring on the rear of the saddle held a coil of rope. The cattleman was in his shirt sleeves. A single suspender was strained with the weight of his pants, which were six inches short of the tops of his brogans, revealing bare ankles. Mounted to his copper-riveted, low-quarter shoes was a pair of heavy iron spurs whose ponderous rowels rattled as he rode. A broad-brimmed straw hat that had "gone to seed" sat on his head. The cattleman carried a branding iron in his right hand bearing the letters *VH*. The reporter immediately thought of Victor Hugo but dismissed the idea.

As they talked, the writer found the cattleman to be intelligent and well informed. He was quite ready to discuss the national and international tariff, mainly because he disagreed with the political philosophy espoused by the correspondent's newspaper. Just as the cattleman broached the topic of national finance, the reporter had to catch a train, but he had no doubt he could have been edified on the subject. He cautioned readers not to jump on a Florida cracker expecting to find a fool.[27]

Much of the Florida cowboy's work was seasonal, including spring and fall roundups, or "cow hunts," and the driving of herds to Gulf ports for shipment by steamer to Cuba and markets in the Florida Keys. Fall roundups were begun in September and lasted about a month. The fat steers were driven to market, leaving better pasture for the remainder of the herd. In the spring, herds were gathered to sort cattle that had mixed on the open range during the winter and assign them to their rightful owners so they could be marked with lawful brands and earmarks. A large part of the roundups involved cow hunting in tangled thickets with the aid of catch dogs. The vicious mongrels were trained to flush cattle out of palmetto clumps and hold them by biting into their nostrils until the cowboys arrived.

Preparations for spring roundups were completed by the middle of March. Large wagons were loaded with provisions,

Cattle branding at the Parker ranch headquarters. (Photo courtesy June Parker Whidden)

Cowboys employed by the King brothers driving cattle near North Island between Palmdale and La Belle. (Photo courtesy H. Logan King, Jr.)

bedding, and feed for four to eight horses. In most cases the mounts were bought from traders who brought them in from Tennessee. A few days ahead of the cowboys, teamsters moved out with the supply wagons to the first cattle pen. Upon arrival, they would butcher a cow or steer, cut the meat into small pieces, season it with salt and red pepper, and then smoke it for consumption at lunchtime during the busy days ahead. Often, however, supply wagons were unable to accompany the cowboys because of restricted travel through swamps, streams, and flooded prairies. In these instances, each cowboy was forced to carry his own supplies with him on his horse. The clothing he had on and the food he carried had to last the entire outing.

Stock tenders slept on the ground. In the wet season, they dug parallel ditches, heaped the dirt in the center, and piled palmetto fans on top of the mound to sleep on, using a poncho for cover. It was not uncommon for the whole crew to be awakened during the night by an unfortunate sleeper rolling over into a water-filled ditch.[28] A calico net over the cowboys kept out sand flies and mosquitos. Smudge fires were built at night to protect the horses from mosquitos that kept them irritable throughout the night. As one local put it, each cowboy had to "ride the buck out of his horse every morning."[29]

Surrounded by woods filled with cattle, the outfit often

Jacob Summerlin, an early Florida cattleman who became known as the "king of the crackers." (Polk County Historical and Genealogical Library, Bartow)

stayed in a camp for ten days or more, cow hunting a radius of about ten miles. Steers were cut out and driven into pens; calves and their mothers were placed in other pens. After the young were branded and marked, they were driven back into the woods with their mothers and left in the same general area where they were found.

The rangelands tended by cowboys expanded gradually but persistently. As the Seminole Indians were pressed ever southward toward the Everglades, Florida cattlemen moved in to take their place. One of these was Jacob Summerlin, who moved into the area to trade slaves for cattle and who became widely known as the "king of the crackers."[30] In 1861 Summerlin arrived in Fort Ogden and secured a two-year contract with the Confederate government to supply steers for the army at ten dollars a head. He drove the steers to Baldwin in the northern part of the state where they were shipped by rail to Georgia and the Carolinas. When Federal troops stopped the northern transport of cattle, Summerlin built a road from Fort Ogden to Punta Rassa, where he and an associate, Captain James McKay, Sr., constructed a wharf and shipping pens to transport cattle to Cuba on clippers and small steamers. Early shipping facilities for the Cuban trade were also constructed on Ballast Point in Old Tampa Bay and at the village of Manatee. Channel conditions at Manatee, however, were less desirable than those at other ports.

Prior to the building of the Summerlin House in 1874, cattlemen used the facilities of the old military barracks of Fort Dulaney, built by the U.S. government at Punta Rassa during the Seminole wars. In late 1866 the International Ocean Telegraph Company took over one room of the building as the Florida terminus for the undersea cable to Cuba, but cattlemen continued to use the accommodations for many years.

Bone Mizell and his fellow cowboys had the difficult, even hazardous, job of driving cattle overland to Punta Rassa. A team of three to five cowboys would round up 300–400 head and drive the herd perhaps 100 miles over the sweeping ranges of DeSoto County. The cattle were driven eight to ten miles each day and herded at night if holding pens were not available. While herding, two of the men were constantly in the saddle on watch until midnight, when they were relieved

Wharf and shipping pens built by Jacob Summerlin in 1874 near the telegraph station at Punta Rassa, Florida. (Photo courtesy Florida Photographic Archives)

by two others who watched the remainder of the night.

Stampedes were not uncommon on the drives to ports, causing considerable loss of cattle, time, and sometimes men. Too much or too little water, depending on the season, was another common problem. During dry seasons, the cattlemen searched for holes wallowed out by alligators in limestone ponds or maiden cane beds where water seeped in, which might be the only usable water for miles. The cowboys first had to drag the alligators out of the holes with ropes and tie them to trees before helping themselves to the water. Often, however, the musk of the disturbed animals rendered the water unusable.[31]

Always a risky venture for the drivers was the tedious crossing of the Caloosahatchee River at one of two places. From the Kissimmee River and other eastern parts of DeSoto County, cattle were driven through open country to the headwaters of the Caloosahatchee. There water poured out of Lake Flirt over a high rock ledge and into the head of the river. During a drought, cattle could wade the ford just below this unusual waterfall, which was destroyed in 1881 by dredging and reclamation projects. But the cascade was completely submerged in wet seasons as water overflowed the riverbanks and spread across the flatlands, making the crossing a mile wide. Cattle could wade through most of the ford but still had

Chute leading to the old cattle crossing on the Caloosahatchee River near Olga. (Photo courtesy Eleanore H. D. Pearse)

to swim over a hundred yards across the riverbed. A half-day was required to complete the crossing, with the cowboys swimming their horses alongside the herds and often returning more than once for supplies. Then, turning southwest, the herds were trailed along the river to holding pens at Fort Denaud, Twelve Mile Creek, Fort Myers, and a final overnight stop a few miles inland from Punta Rassa. With the cattle port in sight, trail herds crossed over a corduroy road that spanned six hundred yards of saltwater bog and quicksand. The walkway was built by pioneer cattlemen who cut pine trees into ten-foot lengths, squared out ten inches of heart pine, and placed the timbers side by side.

The other crossing point of the Caloosahatchee was near Olga, some fifteen miles upstream from Fort Myers. To aid cattle across the river, a ten-by-eighteen-foot scow was operated just above the ford. When the flat-bottomed boat moved across the river, its wake spread across and slightly downstream, the general direction in which herds had a tendency to swim. It was considerably easier for the cattle to swim with

Cattle crossing the Caloosahatchee River at Fort Thompson. In the dry season, cattle could wade through most of the ford.

the surge of the swells than laterally to a buffeting current. From the south side of the ford, cattle were then trailed down the general course of the river to the old corduroy road and into Punta Rassa.

The shipping pens at Punta Rassa held about 800 cattle, the maximum number that could be transported by the largest ship in the Cuban trade. After their arrival at the port, the animals were loaded as soon as possible to avoid weight loss. Amid the pandemonium of clattering hoofs, shouting cowboys, cracking whips, and barking dogs, the wild-eyed cattle were driven from the yards to the ship along a narrow passageway boarded on both sides. At the end of the wharf, the bawling cattle huddled together, penning themselves. A noose was cast over the horns of each animal, and one at a time they were yanked from the wharf to the ship by means of a block and tackle operating from a spar. When the storage below deck was filled with struggling animals, the remainder of the herd was forced aboard the upper deck through strong loading chutes.[32] One observer described the bedlam this way: "The task is a tedious one, and when carried on at night in the light of pitch-pine torches throwed a wild, red glare on the rough bearded faces, tossing horns and hoofs; the piratical looking schooner and her Spanish crew, amid bellowing brutes and men it was wild and picturesque."[33]

Cuban ports of entry for Florida cattle were Havana, Sague

La Grande, and Nuivetes. Steamships like the *Lizzie Henderson* and the *Eda Knight* could carry 300 to 500 head of cattle, depending upon the size of the animals. An even larger number of cattle could be shipped on the Cuban *Guillermo*. The average price for cattle at Punta Rassa was $14 per head, with cattlemen absorbing wharfage and causeway expenses. Spanish gold became the medium of exchange for Florida cattlemen.

After the Cuban rebellion against Spain in 1881, a duty of six dollars per head and a transportation tax of five dollars per head were levied on imported cattle from Florida, which led to a drastic curtailment in shipments to Cuban markets by 1883. However, shipments were soon revived at Punta Rassa by a demand for slaughter cattle at Key West brought about by a boom in cigar production and the start of a sponge fishing industry. But when Tampa became the center for cigar manufacturing and new sponge fishing grounds were discovered off Tarpon Springs, the shipment of cattle by boat from Punta Rassa ended.

Bone Mizell survived the dangers, if not the excesses, of the cowboy's life and witnessed many changes in Florida's cattle industry. He was both an ordinary cowboy and the voice of an era. He left his mark on the early Florida cattle industry, although admittedly it was sometimes on the hides of cattle that belonged to someone else.

5

"Larceny of domestic animals, to wit, steers"

"This became so general at one time around Arcadia many owners of cattle entered into a compact and signed an agreement to the effect that from the date of the instrument all cattle thefts should cease."

Bone Mizell and other cattlemen lived through tumultuous and dangerous times in the early days of Florida's cattle industry. These dangers were not confined to the usual occupational hazards of stock tending. The far-flung cattle ranges of old DeSoto County, covering what is now five counties, were the setting for Florida's infamous range wars, rustling activities, and related murders and other acts of violence that went on from the creation of the county almost up to the year of Bone's death in 1921. As late as World War I, cattlemen around Arcadia kept their shades drawn at night and walked on the far side of house lights so their shadows would not fall on window curtains, thereby reducing the possibility of being shot in their homes. During the day they avoided thick cabbage palm hammocks and dense woods that might harbor danger.[1] When cowboys slept out at night, the cautious ones bedded down with their heads away from tree trunks so their feet would be the gunshot target of vengeful rustlers.[2]

Contemporary accounts of the DeSoto County cattle wars are

scarce. Area newspapers were few and far between, and their editors often chose not to write about these matters out of fear for their personal safety and because of the widespread involvement of influential citizens. Arcadia newspaper coverage, if any existed, is lost forever. On Thanksgiving Day in 1905, a devastating fire swept through the town and completely destroyed forty wooden structures, including the newspaper office with its back issues, files, and diaries. Only three businesses, those housed in brick buildings, were saved.

Some history can be reconstructed from the memories of a few older Floridians and descendants of those who participated in the cattle wars, and a few unpublished memoirs, papers, and notes still exist. Old court records are one of the best sources of information about the cattle wars. The first book of minutes for DeSoto County Circuit Court, covering the period from 1887 to 1900, is dominated by criminal cases involving larceny of domestic animals, fraudulent alteration of brands, carrying concealed weapons, assault with intent to murder, first-degree mur-

Cracker Cowboys of Florida *by Frederic Remington. (Originally reproduced in* Harper's New Monthly Magazine, *August 1895)*

der, and selling spirituous liquor in violation of local option laws.

We do know that frontier violence was a way of life in the area even before DeSoto County was created from Manatee County in 1887. Widely publicized at the time was a vigilante action between land-grabbers (speculators) and homesteaders in 1884–85 that resulted in as many as eight brutal murders.[3] Others less directly involved in the confrontation considered an ultimatum issued by the vigilantes and left the country. The incident grew out of competition for landownership in the state. Property was readily available for homesteading until 1883, when almost all land in the public domain was sold to speculators by the Florida Internal Improvement Board, which was eager to develop transportation and free the state from debt. Strangely allied with the land-grabbers were a few prominent cattlemen who sought to prevent homesteaders from encroaching on the open range. Land agents quickly began ouster proceedings on settlers already established and threatened their immediate eviction. Enraged by these developments, seventeen pioneers met secretly in early April 1884 and formed what they called the Sara Sota Vigilance Committee, or the SSVC.

The unauthorized group was governed by two "judges," one "captain," and three "lieutenants," who ruled with an iron hand. The penalty imposed against a member for absence from any three meetings was a whipping with stirrup leather as the guilty party bent over a log; the group's watchword was Death to All Traitors. Committee members were secretly sworn to take care of each other by an oath that read in part: "I do of my own free will and accord, etc., protect and sustain any member of this band *be he in the right or in the wrong.*"[4]

Following a brief but bloody reign of terror throughout the county, twenty vigilantes were arrested and brought to trial in May 1885; two more trials were held in July and August. Scores of heavily armed men camped near the courthouse in Pine Level to see that justice was done one way or another. Only seven of the defendants were found guilty of first-degree murder, and even though some were sentenced to be hanged, none suffered the full penalty for his crime. A few of the vigilantes escaped, and the others were released within a few years.[5]

The first criminal case scheduled in DeSoto County after its formation reflected the violence associated with the early cattle

Jesse Bolivar Mizell, Bone's brother and sheriff of Manatee County, who was slain in a cow camp. (Sebring Historical Society)

industry. The case involved Jess Mizell, Bone's brother, and Marion Platt, a successful and respected cattleman. Both men became victims of the violent times in which they lived. On June 10, 1884, Marion Platt, Fines Parker, Alfred Williams, D. S. Moray, and Jess Mizell were working cattle at David Waldron's pens near Fort Thompson when a heated dispute arose. By the time the men had their evening meal, tempers seemed to have cooled. The next day, the group moved to W. S. Clay's cattle pens.

According to Platt, "a third-party busybody" restarted the argument as the men were passing around a flask of rum. Amid charges and countercharges of letting each other's cattle out of pens, guns came into play, and Platt shot and killed Jess Mizell.[6] The only eyewitness was twelve-year-old Nick Langford, Jr., who remained on the scene after the other cowboys had ridden off. The youth stated that Jess was trying to make peace between Platt and Owen Morey, a brother-in-law of Jess and Bone Mizell.[7] For Platt the incident was the worst moment of his life. He later wrote that it "caused women and children to weep, the old and young to grieve, friends to be enemies, money spent and land sacrificed."[8]

Chief Deputy Owen H. Dishong, who had served under Jess Mizell when the latter was sheriff of Manatee County, investigated the incident. After questioning witnesses, he rode back to the Platt home in Pine Level seeking the whereabouts of Francis Marion Platt. The cattleman's wife, the former Annie Mizell and a first cousin of the man her husband shot, could only tell the deputy with honesty that Platt had stopped by long enough to tell her he was on his way to "Californee." In fact, Platt was spirited away by night to an oak and cabbage hammock in the Bay Galls, an extensive wilderness south of Lake Istokpoga between Arcadia and Okeechobee. Cowboys working for the prominent Parker family saw to it that supplies reached Platt from time to time. When one would return to the ranch he would comment that he had been on a little trip to "Californee." The place has been known as Californee Hammock ever since.[9]

While in hiding, Platt scouted out a chain of islands with fine grazing areas in the Bay Galls. He gave their whereabouts to the Parkers with the warning that bears could be a problem. The Parkers sent a cowboy crew to build log pens and drive a large herd of cattle into the area. During the first night bears killed or crippled eleven steers. In the next three weeks, Platt and Parker cowboys killed thirty-three bears.

After a lonely year in the Bay Galls, Platt was smuggled to Tampa, where he hid out on a fruit boat and sailed to Central America. He later decided to return home and stand trial. Back in Arcadia, he was indicted for first-degree murder, and a trial date was set for the 1888 spring term, the first criminal trial scheduled in newly formed DeSoto County. The case was contin-

A Bit of Cow Country *by Frederic Remington. (Originally reproduced in* Harper's New Monthly Magazine, *August 1895)*

ued. The following spring the case was continued again when witnesses failed to appear, for which they were each fined $50. The case was finally brought to trial during the fall term, and on September 18, 1889, a jury returned a verdict of not guilty in favor of Platt.[10] In the fall of 1898, Platt moved across the state into the backwoods near the east coast, becoming the first settler in the area. He helped carve out of the wilderness the community of Indiantown, which he originally named Annie in honor of his wife.[11]

A frequent spark in the DeSoto County range wars was unbranded cattle. Virtually free plunder, they were branded by anyone who found them. Some cattlemen were herding and marking all the cattle they could chase out of the hammocks and scrub, even if the animals already carried ownership marks. Calves were often branded by whoever found them regardless of who owned the cows they were following. The older calves without brands or mothers were called "heredics"[12] or "hairydicks,"[13] either phonetic spelling a refinement or corruption of the other. All this had a demoralizing effect on cowboys in the ranchers' employ, who began to register their own brands and mark cattle for themselves.

The biggest ranchers were not disturbed by, and no doubt even expected, a minor loss of cattle to families who needed beef for food. But a wholesale branding and marketing of their stock led to armed resistance throughout the county. Heavily armed men patrolled the ranges for their bosses, enforcing a brand of justice that was swift and complete. If retaliation followed, the rustler or enforcer simply fled into the unknown reaches of the Everglades. A former cowboy confided to Frederic Remington that in the vast wilderness "a boat don't leave no trail, stranger."[14] The number of men shot or hanged and left on the spot will never be known. On one occasion, two rival foremen rode hell-bent toward each other, firing pointblank. Both were found dying in the palmettos, one calling out the name of his boss.

Because of their unusual method of operation, it was difficult

Cowboys Wrestling a Bull *by Frederic Remington. (Originally repro-duced in* Harper's New Monthly Magazine, *August 1895)*

to prosecute cattle thieves in DeSoto County. A rustler with cattle to sell could always present a clean bill of sale and offer an official record of ownership. In many cases the rustler had bought the stock from another cattle thief, that thief from another, and on down a chain of illegal owners. When one was caught, he could clear himself with his records. The previous owner could do likewise, and so on down through successive owners. By the time the end of the chain was reached, the first thief had heard of the troubles in court and was nowhere to be found.[15] Wholesale and retail cattle markets flourished along with the thievery. Butchers knew they were safe in buying "hot" beef and could set their own purchase price. Stolen cattle arrived with their brands burned out and their ears completely cut off so ownership could not be established. Whoever brought the cattle to market got paid.[16]

Around 1890 four rustlers made off with 200 head of cattle near Arcadia and got as far as Titusville. A posse of twenty cattlemen gave chase and recovered the stolen herd after a brief gun battle. Two of the rustlers were killed in the encounter, and the remaining two were quickly disposed of by the posse.[17] Some members of a gang of rustlers were captured in 1894, but they made their escape before coming to trial.

To make up their losses, many prominent ranchers honestly engaged in the cattle industry finally resorted to rustling in self-defense.[18] A few DeSoto County cattlemen began to drive all the stock they could to their own pastures. If they were missing cattle, they simply raided stock from the most convenient pastures. Many herds had been branded and rebranded so often that the marks were indecipherable, and the cattle were sold several times for as little as two dollars per head. Honest cattlemen suffered heavy losses and stationed guards around their pastures with instructions to protect their property at all costs. On July 19, 1895, a Jacksonville newspaper printed a story out of Fort Ogden with the headline "Cattle Kings to Clash," warning that open warfare among the major ranchers was imminent.[19] One rancher estimated that between 1891 and 1896, 3,000 head of cattle belonging to him and his friends were stolen on DeSoto County ranges.[20] In a four-week period during the summer of 1896, Ziba King recovered 2,500 head of his stolen cattle.[21]

In 1896 cattle owners Bob Whidden, Buck King, and William Hooker trailed a band of rustlers who had stolen a hand-picked

In Wait for an Enemy *by Frederic Remington. (Originally reporduced in* Harper's New Monthly Magazine, *August 1895)*

herd of 300 steers and drove them to an Orlando slaughter-house. There the cattlemen found branded hides of some of the cattle, but the main herd was nowhere to be found. Enraged, the men rode south to Kissimmee where they were joined by the sheriff of Osceola County and two deputies. The reinforced party continued on to Canoe Creek where the outlaws had crossed a boggy marsh with the stolen herd. Tying blankets to the feet of their horses to keep them from miring in the muck, the deter-mined posse made the crossing into Polk County, where they were joined by the Lykes foreman and some of his cowboys. A short distance from the Lykes ranch headquarters, they caught up with the thieves. A gun battle broke out; the cattle were recov-ered and the surviving raiders captured. Another posse of ten ranchers from Manatee County, pursuing the same cow thieves, arrived on the scene just after the capture. The rustlers were each given five years for stealing cattle and another five years for altering brands.[22]

Fighting over a Stolen Herd *by Frederic Remington. (Originally repro-*
duced in Harper's New Monthly Magazine, *August 1895)*

The unlawful altering or defacing of cattle brands was common during the range wars. Frederic Remington recalled that in
Arcadia, an intoxicated cowboy well schooled in destroying legal
brands took a pencil from him and displayed his craft on a sheet
of wrapping paper. Whether deliberately or by chance, the cowboy drew an ordinary circle, part of the Circle O brand registered
by Ziba King. "This brand is no good," declared the cowboy as
he altered it by drawing a ring around the circle. Using another
oval, he placed the numeral 1 in front to form a Ten brand. Then
he placed an *E* in front of another circle and continued the middle line of the letter through the circle, halving it to form a distinctive brand. To make a Circle Cross brand, he simply placed
a cross in the center of a newly drawn circle. Completing his les-
son in brand altering, the clever designer drew four spokes inside another circle, extending each spoke outside the circle and
bending the ends slightly in the same direction. "Make the
damned thing whirl," explained the obviously proud artist.[23]

Ziba King's Circle O brand was frequently altered. On one indictment in 1896, King charged that two defendants illegally
claimed some of his cattle by inserting a small heart inside his
brand.[24]

As a judge, King was actively engaged in prosecuting rustlers and consequently became one of their main assassination targets. Another prominent cattle owner in DeSoto County asserted his rights and had sixteen buckshot pumped into him while he was bent over a spring to drink. He lived and left the county voluntarily.[25]

A close call between cattle owners and rustlers involved Eli

Colonel Eli O. Morgan, a prominent Florida cattle owner, in 1900. (Photo courtesy John T. Lesley)

Morgan and his son-in-law E. L. (Sonny) Lesley as they drove a herd of cattle from the Kissimmee River to Fort Thompson. Morgan had been involved in many suits against rustlers. It rained the whole eight days of the drive, and they were in water ankle- to waist-deep all the way. At night they would search out a high hammock, cut palmetto fans, and place them around tree trunks to build sleeping places up out of the water. They risked sharing their makeshift beds with water moccasins, but the real danger on the trip was yet to come.

On their return home, Morgan and Lesley stopped at a small store near Fish Eating Creek, where they spotted the tracks of two horses that had been ridden up to the store after a rain the night before. The riders had turned and headed back in the same direction they had come. The proprietor did not know the strangers, but from his description Lesley was sure of their iden- tity and the probable nature of their mission. Morgan also knew the riders, though he did not mention this fact to Lesley. He got out his shotgun and some shells and kept the weapon in his hands for the remainder of the trip.

Lesley later wrote that he had never experienced such a sen- sation as he did while crossing the Saw Grass, an eight-mile prairie spotted with palmetto clumps. The trail seemed to run up to the fringe of every clump and swing around it. Lesley fully expected to be shot each time they approached the palmettos. "But we made it through," he wrote, "and sometime later in con- versation with one of the men I thought rode one of the horses, he told me very frankly that he was one of them and that they had ridden around us at least three times trying to get a shot at Mr. Morgan without hitting me. During this ride neither of us mentioned what was in our thoughts and both expected to get shot every few minutes."[26]

Lesley later became a cattle king in his own right in Osceola County. Rustling was not as common on the east side of the Kissimmee River as it was on the west side, however, and the Lesley cowboys were instructed to do their best to keep every- thing with an altered brand from crossing over from DeSoto County.

There were numerous indictments in the early days of DeSoto County for placing obstructions on railroad tracks and shooting into railway cars. Range cattle that wandered onto the tracks

E. L. (Sonny) Lesley, Colonel Morgan's son-in-law, in 1910. (Photo courtesy John T. Lesley)

were frequently struck and killed by trains, and when this happened cattlemen demanded quick settlement from the railroad company, often at gunpoint. At first the company refused to pay the extremely high price cattlemen placed on their losses, but when cowboys began to attack trains and pump bullets into passenger cars, the company was forced to hire an adjuster, locally called a "cow attorney."[27] During his stay in Florida, Frederic Remington wrote a letter in February 1895 to his friend Owen Wister in Philadelphia, inviting the novelist down to Arcadia and Punta Gorda. One of the attractions he wanted his friend to see was "curious cowboys who shoot up railroad trains."[28]

On March 18, 1888, eight crossties were placed across the tracks of the "fast mail" and set on fire within fifty feet of Bridge No. 50 south of Zolfo. Two nights later, the same train was delayed twenty-five minutes while another fire was brought under control and obstructions removed from Bridge No. 49. The incidents were denounced in an area newspaper nine days later: "The foundation of it all is probably a petty squabble as to the value of the cattle killed by the railroad and in no case does the difference exceed a dollar or two."[29]

If these difficulties weren't enough, there were also a number of desperados who traveled in and out of DeSoto County during those lawless years. One was Hub Williams, who called himself the Robin Hood of Florida because he claimed to rob from the rich and give to the poor. Williams was involved in a humorous but potentially explosive incident initiated by a man named George Mansfield near Arcadia. Mansfield had moved to Fort Ogden from Tennessee. While looking for a job he met Bone Mizell, who was then working for Ziba King. Bone advised Mansfield that he might get a job with the Parkers. The newcomer walked north to the Parker headquarters and hired on as a cowboy.

One Saturday afternoon a couple of years later, Mansfield and another cowboy, Jim Bates, decided to attend a dance being held at a farmhouse several miles away. After about an hour of riding in their ox cart, nipping at a bottle along the way, the two spied an approaching rider. Feeling full of foolishness, Mansfield decided to pretend to be the well-known Hub Williams. The three met and passed the time of day. Suddenly Mansfield pulled his gun, identified himself as the noted desperado, and told the rider to dismount and start dancing. Quite literally under the gun, the stranger danced for thirty minutes before he was allowed to stop. After his exhausting ordeal, the dancer told the cowboys that he had two quarts of good whiskey in his saddlebags and would be glad for them to share it. The cowboys readily agreed.

Reaching into his saddlebags, the unidentified rider pulled out a pistol and announced, "Boys, you are now looking at the real Hub Williams." Turning to Mansfield he continued, "You and your friend step right over here where I have been dancing, and I mean pick 'em up and lay 'em down." Williams kept the two cowboys dancing until they were so tired they could hardly stand. Then, after firing several shots in the air to scare their oxen, he mounted his horse and went on his way. Mansfield and Bates ran on foot to catch up with their team.[30]

Hub Williams was finally captured and tried in Tampa in 1874 for horse stealing. He was convicted and sentenced to the state penitentiary by Judge James T. Magbee, but on the way to prison Williams escaped. He was never recaptured, and he became so dangerous that men were ready to commit murder to be rid of him. According to local tradition, a plot was laid to kill him in Brooksville one night. Surrounded by a band of armed men that called themselves Regulators, Hub realized the futility of a fight and began to walk away. The Regulators then opened fire with shotguns, rifles, and pistols. One clubbed the bullet-ridden fugitive with a shotgun butt when he refused to die. Although the owner of the shotgun left beside the dying Williams was easily identified and most of the attackers were well known, there were no convictions.[31]

An area newspaper gave a different account of Hub's death that was far less of an indictment against the Regulators. According to this version, John W. Williams, generally known as Hub Williams, started the deadly shooting himself. Williams had resorted to his old ways by firing into a group of men, who returned the fire and mortally wounded the outlaw on the night of February 24, 1880. He died of his wounds the next morning.[32] By the time of the shooting, James Magbee, the judge who had sentenced Hub, was owner and editor of his own Tampa newspaper. Three days after Williams died, Magbee commented in a brief account of the incident: "We understand that 'Hub' Williams was shot and killed by unknown parties in Hernando County. Hub has been recently pardoned for crimes for which he was committed, and now has come to the sad end above. Poor Hub!"[33]

Another notorious fugitive, called a "well-known desperado" by the Bartow newspaper, was Quinn Bass. He was shot and killed near Arcadia on May 29, 1894, five months after his escape from the Arcadia jail where he was serving a life sentence for murder.

While he was still at large, Sheriff F. C. Bethea discovered that Bass had an engagement to meet a woman at Coon Prairie about a mile and a half out of town. He deputized four men to assist in arresting the fugitive. The posse concealed themselves at the meeting place and waited for their man, who rode up shortly thereafter. Passing the sheriff and his group, Bass dismounted, tied up his horse, and began walking beside a fence. While doing so, he caught a glimpse of the lawmen lying on the ground and went for his pistol. One member of the posse yelled for Bass to throw up his hands, but instead the wanted man began firing. A volley of gunfire was returned by the lawmen. Bass turned, ran a short distance, and fell dead, riddled with bullets and buckshot.[34]

Cattle rustling and rum running became closely allied, heightening the danger of both operations. Many rustlers found it profitable to produce illegal whiskey, and as the production of moonshine became more competitive some bootleggers took up cattle stealing. The combined ventures led to numerous gun battles and killings. Unlike Bone Mizell, who was comical and friendly when drinking, many cowboys became edgy and dangerous under the influence. Drinking parties often ended in fights or shotgun duels.

Back Johnson was a near fatality of one cow camp drinking party. Back, who dropped the *t* in the family name Johnston because it sounded "high falutin'," was a close friend of Bone's and had sold him a herd of cattle in 1892. On July 1, 1896, Back and a group of young cowboys were camped by Fish Eating Creek forty miles east of Arcadia. Among them was Joe Peebles, a former tax collector at Punta Gorda whose father was one of the largest stock owners in the state. Back had been in charge of Ziba King's slaughterhouse in Punta Gorda for a number of years. A whiskey dealer rode into the camp with a supply of rum, and the cowboys began to imbibe. A row developed, and Back was stabbed twice in the abdomen and once in the head and back by Joe Peebles. A man named Bryant shot the assailant in the legs. It was believed the knife wounds would prove fatal to Back; a press report even called the affray a murder.[35] However,

Back eventually recovered and lived until 1938. He probably would not have survived the fight if Jim Peebles, the assailant's brother, had not sewn up his wounds.[36]

By the late 1890s, cattle rustling and its attendant crimes had become so prevalent in DeSoto County that the area's major ranchers, some of whom had been drawn into criminal activity themselves, began a concerted effort to stop the lawlessness. Ziba King got a court order from Judge Barron Phillips to round up all cattle bearing altered or defaced brands, sell them, and then apportion the proceeds among the cattle's legal owners. However, legal ownership was so difficult to prove that the cattlemen got together and called off the plan because the only ones to profit were the wholesale and retail markets.[37]

Citrus grower and cattleman James Newton (Jim) Hollingsworth, in an attempt to get the ranchers to cooperate, wanted them to separate cattle by their brands and to establish

James Newton Hollingworth, DeSoto County cattleman, is credited with getting rival cattlemen together in 1896 to combat widespread rustling in the county. (Courtesy of Louise Frisbie)

calf ownership by "mothering." This technique depended on the fact that because each cow knew her own calf and each calf knew its own mother, they would eventually get together if allowed the chance to do so. Older calves that had been overlooked in previous roundups would be divided among the cattlemen as equally as possible.[38] Hollingsworth warned that if the rustling did not stop, "everybody is going to get killed and the cattle will still be here."[39]

On May 6, 1896, a group of prominent cattlemen met in Arcadia to combat the wretched state of cattle interests throughout DeSoto County. Conditions were becoming intolerable. Rustlers were rebranding cattle by effacing the original brands and lopping off the animals' ears to remove the earmarks. Disfigured cattle with altered and defaced brands were to be found all over the ranges; only a week before the meeting, 700 such cattle were turned into one pasture. The *Florida Times-Union* in Jacksonville reported on the outcome of the lengthy meeting: "At midnight a conclusion was reached, and every cattle owner present signed a pledge not to steal cattle himself, hire no one else to do it for him, nor suffer any other man to do it if he could help it. Further not to buy, sell, or handle such stock; nor go on any man's bond who may do any or all these things. Affirmatively they pledged themselves to use every effort to punish cattle thieves in the county by rendering the courts every possible aid in prosecution."[40] A year later, the same newspaper stated that signing this peculiar document was almost a tacit admission of the cattlemen's participation in the lawlessness. Fortunately, wholesale larceny of cattle ended with the signing of this agreement.[41] From then on, rustling was more or less confined to isolated instances that probably did not involve the major cattle owners.

Like most other cattlemen of his time, Bone Mizell was not immune to the lawlessness of the era. There were a number of charges against him for rustling cattle, altering brands, and marking unmarked cattle and hogs. He was open, even boastful, about his part in these illegal activities, and his friends often did not know whether he was kidding or being serious. For example, just after Ed Welles and Katherine Whidden were married, they lived on the west side of the Peace River. One day Ed jokingly said to Bone, "My wife's alone tonight, so I hope there'll be no trouble over there." "Don't worry," Bone answered, "I'm not working that side of the river tonight."[42]

One of the most well-known stories about Bone's cattle larceny involved a judge fictitiously named Colonel Zuigg in Frederic Remington's illustrated account of cracker cowboys. Remington was in Florida in early 1895 researching his article, and he interviewed an Arcadia banker who had once been a cowboy himself. During their conversation, a "bull hunter" who had obviously been drinking approached the banker and asked for a $20 advance on his boss's credit. The odd transaction was quickly made with no questions asked. When the cowboy left, a perplexed Remington asked the banker if the employer had authorized this instant loan service for his cowboys. "I gave some money to some of his boys some weeks ago," the banker replied, "and when the colonel was down here, I asked him if he wanted the boys to draw against him in that way. He said, 'Yes—for a small amount; they will steal a cow or two, and pay me that way.'" The cowboy's employer became Colonel Zuigg in Remington's article, no doubt to prevent embarrassment or perhaps a lawsuit. The colonel had once served as a judge and had decided a case against the Arcadia banker. The judge had explained his decision by saying that he had decided the last eight cases in the banker's favor and it wasn't right for him to have it his way all the time.

This same judge, the so-called Colonel Zuigg, once had Bone indicted for stealing cattle. (Although in Remington's account the cowboy is named Zorn Zuidden, the protagonist is unmistakably Bone Mizell. This particular instance of Bone's getting the last word was well known before the article was published.) "Now see here," Bone reasoned with the judge, "what do you want to go and get me arrested for? I have stole thousands of cattle and put your mark and brand on them, and just because I have stole a couple of hundred from you, you go and have me indicted. You just better go and get that whole deal nol-prossed."[43] According to Remington's account and oral history, that is precisely what happened.

Court records indicate that on March 17, 1893, Bone was indicted in DeSoto County Criminal Court for larceny of domestic animals. A year later a jury found him innocent. Two days after the verdict, Bone was again indicted for rustling a cow; the case was later nol-prossed. On the same day, March 16, 1894, Bone was charged in two more cow larceny cases and with rustling steers in another case. It was three years before these cases were disposed of; Bone was acquitted in one case, and the other two cases were nol-prossed.[44]

In 1894 Bone was also indicted for driving cattle out of DeSoto County without having marks and brands properly exhibited or inspected. On February 13, 1895, Judge A. E. Pooser ruled that the charge be "quashed on hearing motion of defendant's counsel." Another indictment on March 15, 1895, charged Bone with larceny of a cow.[45] The trial was set for the following spring, but by then Bone was in serious trouble in neighboring Lee County. On March 2, 1896, in Fort Myers, he was found guilty of cattle stealing and sentenced to two years at hard labor in the state penitentiary.[46] Meanwhile, back in Arcadia, the spring term of the Circuit Court for DeSoto County opened with four cases against Bone for larceny of domestic animals. The following disposition was entered in the court minutes on March 9, 1896: "Continued because the defendant has been convicted of larceny in Lee County and is in the State Penitentiary."[47]

A Pine Level resident who knew members of the Lee County

DeSoto County's first jail (left) and courthouse in 1895, the year Bone was a frequent visitor. (Photo courtesy of George Lane, Jr.)

jury later recalled Bone's conviction and the unusual events that followed. The general belief at the time was that he had been stealing for a cattle king.

The trial jury was locked up for one night on the second floor of the courthouse with guards stationed at the door of the room and the building entrances. Around ten o'clock that evening, a rock tied to a line was thrown through a window into the jury room. A note tied to the rock gave instructions to pull on the line. A rope was found attached to the end of the line, and tied to the other end of the rope was a large basket filled with food, liquor, and cigars. But despite this attempt by someone on Bone's side to influence the jury, Bone was found guilty.

Before commitment papers had been completed, a petition for Bone's pardon was circulated in Arcadia, but his many supporters were told the request could not be granted until Bone had actually served time. So they outfitted him in new clothes, escorted him to the train station, and gave him a sendoff worthy of a hero.

Arriving at the state prison, Bone found that his reputation had preceded him. He was met by a prison official who personally conducted him on a tour of the institution and invited him to dinner. After the meal Bone showed his appreciation by giving an impromptu speech in which he said he found no fault with the management. Thus, having "served time" in the penitentiary, Bone boarded the next train home.[48]

In the fall of 1896, Bone helped a friend out of a legal skirmish similar to one of his own. The friend was arrested for butchering a cow of questionable ownership. Although he was well known in DeSoto County as an upstanding citizen, he was worried about his upcoming trial. Bone made him an offer: "You buy me a John B. Stetson hat, and I'll get you out of this in two minutes," he said. "How?" asked the friend. "Just have them call me as a witness," Bone answered. The cowboy agreed.

At the trial, various witnesses were questioned about earmarks, brands, time of day, and other facts concerning the case. Bone was put on the stand and testified that he had seen the alleged butchering. When asked where he was at the time, he replied, "Bee Branch." "Where's Bee Branch?" queried the prosecutor. "Everybody knows where Bee Branch is," answered Bone. "It's two or three hundred yards over in the next county." The defense called for a dismissal on the grounds that the defendant could not be tried in Arcadia for an offense committed in an adjoining county. The case was thrown out of court, and Bone got his new Stetson.[49]

In the spring of 1897, Bone was tried on one of the four charges pending against him in DeSoto County. The jury found the defendant not guilty, and on a motion of State Attorney W. A. Carter, the other three charges were dropped.[50]

On November 27, 1913, five indictments were filed against Bone: two for larceny of hogs, one for grand larceny, one for marking unmarked hogs, and one for altering hog marks. But on April 30, 1914, a jury found him innocent of all the charges.[51] Martha Kreider worked as a scribe for Clerk John Hugh Alford in the DeSoto County Courthouse. She held this position at the young age of fourteen because of her exceptional handwriting skills. Her main duty was to copy court records into the permanent books, and many of these records involved Bone Mizell. Kreider later recalled, "He appeared in my record many times under the indictments for 'larceny of a domestic animal, to wit, a cow' but he told us once that the only time he was convicted was the only time he was not guilty."[52]

There was yet another source of conflict and lawlessness in the cattle industry of those days. Florida's vast prairies, with DeSoto County in the center, were more suitable for stock raising than other forms of agriculture. Accustomed as they were to unlimited free grazing for their stock, cattle owners resented the introduction of barbed wire by agriculturalists and complained bitterly about the enclosure of free pasturage. As early as 1883, some cattlemen were cutting the wire fencing that hindered movement of their ranging stock. But the worst was yet to come, only a year and a half before Bone died.

Around 1919 the American Agricultural Chemical Company began introducing purebred bulls to improve the quality of their cattle. To conserve the services of the males and to keep their cattle tick free, the company fenced in thousands of acres where range cattle had once grazed at will. Cattlemen who had always used the property as free range immediately voiced their objections and threatened to destroy the fence. In early January 1920, the cutting of several miles of the company fence was reported to Sheriff John Logan of Polk County. An investigation turned up no guilty parties. One night later that month, another section of the fence was cut at every other post for several miles.

The next night, the sheriff and his party were on the scene. More cuttings were made but in an area not patrolled by the officers. On the following night, January 29, the sheriff and his deputies returned, but this time they organized themselves in three groups. Two deputies, some five miles south of Brewster, put their ears to the fence and caught the sound of cutting as the offenders approached. When the cutters were within thirty yards of them, one of the deputies called out, "I am a deputy sheriff—I've got the drop on you, boys. Put your hands up."

The lawman immediately dropped to his knees as a charge of buckshot passed over his head, a move that probably saved his life. He and the other officer opened fire, instantly killing the man who had fired the shotgun. The other fence cutters began shooting, and when the smoke cleared, T. W. (Tinker Tom) Albritton, his brother A. J. (Shan) Albritton, and their brother-in-law Niram D. Alderman lay dead on the ground. Neither deputy was hit. The Albrittons' nephew Jasper dropped his gun and fled on foot, running directly into the hands of another party of officers some distance down the fence line. He offered no resistance when taken into custody.[53] The fence cutters were all prosperous stock farmers.

Inevitably, unlimited free range for Florida cattle on land that had no legal title and was often acquired and held by force began to dwindle. Frontier cattle-raising methods that sanctioned fence cuttings, murder, and gunpoint justice were incompatible with modern agriculture. Writing about the Brewster tragedy, an editorial writer in the *Tampa Daily Times* speculated on January 31, 1920, that "the future of the cattle business in Florida will lie within fenced pastures."[54] But a statewide fence law was officially twenty-nine more years in coming.

6

"Stories about him abound"

"To this day when cowpokes rid their beds of pinecone
Near a smouldering fire beyond which mosquitos drone,
Panthers scream, owls hoot, and nervous cows low and moan,
They will bring to mind stories of old cowboy 'Bone.'"

Folktales have lives of their own: They are born of legend and fact, they change with their retelling over the years, they are gradually subsumed in lore that takes their place, or they may die out altogether. Such is the case with the stories told of Bone Mizell. Bone was known throughout the state as a top cowhand, but his pranks and exploits were what made him a favorite topic of conversation among Florida cowboys, and his reputation grew as he became the central figure of their folk narratives. If the "facts" of a story did not coincide with his actual experience, he willingly adopted the tale's persona and played the role with ease.

Folklore is more concerned with the essence of character and the meaning of experience than with the details of time and place—such incidentals may be relayed inconsistently, if at all. As a dynamic medium of cultural expression, the oral tradition is not always a reliable source for verifying certain kinds of information about the past. In Bone's case, particular details of his life are presented differently in various sources. The surname

Mizelle, for example, is spelled with a final e in some popular early writings about Bone, and a few descendants of his immediate family have retained that spelling. His first name also varies in folktales and written narratives. Bone probably acquired the additional name Napoleon later, and many contemporaries used it instead of his real name, Morgan, thinking perhaps that the name Napoleon should precede the name Bonaparte. In fact, two of his many personal cattle brands included the initials of both first names, and Bone himself sometimes used Napoleon as part of his name.[1] Others know the cowboy as "Bones" Mizell because his hometown newspaper used that name in a feature article about him and because of a famous exploit in which he purposely substituted a friend's bones for someone else's and shipped them to New Orleans because his friend had never had a chance to travel during his lifetime.[2] Even the time and place of Bone's birth are frequently misrepresented. In various print sources, the year of his birth spans two decades, and at least four Florida counties have been cited as his birthplace. His tombstone, donated by friends years after this death, is inscribed with the wrong first initial and year of birth.

These and other inconsistencies notwithstanding, research confirms the substantive accuracy of many of the stories told about Bone. These tales are preserved in the memory of some older Floridians and descendants of those who knew him. Vignettes from written memoirs as well as accounts published during Bone's life are recirculated in today's histories of the era. They are invaluable sources of information about Florida's most popular cowboy and the times in which he lived.

Despite his run-ins with the law, Bone accumulated most of his cattle legally. Every year during spring roundup, Ziba King rewarded the cowhand who put the King brand on the largest number of calves by giving him a few head for himself.[3] In 1892, Bone acquired one of King's cows in an irregular fashion that earned him the reputation of being able to earmark cattle without a knife should the need arise. A cowboy who witnessed the incident described the curious event:

One day I was riding the range with Buck King, the boss, and Bone. A thin old cow was discovered at the edge of a thicket of thornbush. She was a pugnacious old beast, evidently planning Bone's discomfiture. Buck challenged: "Rope her and put your mark on her, and you can have her." Bone accepted the challenge and soon had a rope on the cow's horns. He dismounted quickly with knife in hand, but the old cow was hard to handle. She dragged Bone into the thicket, where he lost his knife and had most of his clothes ripped off by the thorny scrub. He finally emerged a sorry spectacle, dragging his lariat. King chided him on being bested by an old range cow.

"But I put my mark on her," declared Bone.

"How could you mark her? I saw you lose your knife," answered King.

"Marked her with my teeth—just as good as I could have done it with a knife," declared Bone.

We ran the old cow out of the brush and verified Bone's statement—he had put his mark in her ears with his teeth.[4]

One of Bone's good friends was Willie Williams, a cattleman in the Fort Basinger area who later became a schoolteacher, citrus grower, and storekeeper. He had rounded up some cattle to drive to the Fort Pierce market when Bone arrived at the camp and offered to help with the cattle drive. A friend of Willie's wrote down what happened:

The drive started early in the morning. Willie, Bone, Frank Raulerson, and two or three more rode along the old government road leading to Fort Drum, from there to Fort Vinson, where there were cowpens built on the old site. Here they were to spend the night, going on to Fort Pierce the next day.

The cattle were put in the pens, and preparations begun to cook supper. It was in the fall and the country was very dry, most of the ponds mud puddles. Bone said, "Boys, I'll go and get some water for coffee, as I know where a 'gator hole is in a pond over yonder."

With a gallon syrup bucket he started out. The others were busy feeding the horses, and Willie began frying bacon and watching a pot of grits, using water from a canteen. When the meat was fried, a can of tomatoes was poured into the grease in the fry pan. Buttermilk bis-

Thomas Butler (Buck) King, son of Ziba King. Bone once accompanied him on a business trip to New York. (Florida Photographic Archives, Tallahassee)

cuits and baked sweet potatoes were taken from the saddlebags. Everything was ready to eat—and no Bone, and no coffee.

He finally came back and said, "Boys, I'm telling you something. I just saw the dangest cat fight I ever saw in my life. On the edge of that flag pond two old bobcats was fighting and growling at one another. All at once they stood up facing each other like two men slapping and growling at one another. Then, like a streak of lightning they clinched and began to climb one another. And so you know what, boys? I stood right there and watched them climb clear out of sight."

Willie said, "Yes, Bone, another one of your tales. Put the water on for coffee."

At daybreak the drive again started for Fort Pierce. The sale completed, rations were bought and all started home. They camped at the same spot on their way home. Bone said, "Boys, I'll go get water for coffee." Willie cautioned him, "Don't be gone so long this time."

Pretty soon Bone was back with the water. One of the boys wanted to rib Bone a little bit. He said, "Bone, did you see anything of your bobcats this trip?" Bone replied, "No boys, but I guess they are still a'fighting, as the fur is still a'falling."[5]

Bone once sold an ox to Zeb Parker, son of Jasper Newton Parker, for $40. Zeb asked him if that wasn't "pretty much money" and Bone told him it was "pretty much steer." The price established, Zeb told Bone to put the animal in his lot, then purposely walked off without paying for the steer. Glancing back to see Bone's reaction, he asked, "Oh, was you waiting to get paid?" With a smile the cowboy replied, "Well, Zeb, that's the part of this here deal I was *particular* interested in."[6]

Bone's skill as a cowboy was legendary. One day he and some of the Kings were driving a herd of wild cattle back to the ranch headquarters when a young bull broke away and disappeared into the thicket. The cowboys searched for the animal but finally gave up and went on with the rest of the herd. Only Bone stayed behind, still looking for the bull.

Around three o'clock the next morning, Bone rode in with the lost bull and enough yelling, whistling, and bellowing to waken the rest of the crew. When asked how he found his way back in the pitch dark, Bone implied that he and the bull navigated their way together: "Well, I'd drive him for a while, and then he'd drive me for a while."[7]

The work Bone did best and enjoyed most was as a cow-hand, a fact he freely admitted. Between roundups the Kings deliberately kept him busy on the ranch to prevent him from getting into trouble in Arcadia. One morning Buck King went to town, leaving Bone with a file and hoe and instructions to dig up the grass from around a grove of orange trees. When Buck returned about midday, Bone had hoed just enough space around one tree to lie down and go to sleep. When asked why he hadn't done more, Bone answered, "I decided I wasn't much of an agriculturist."[8]

Bone's success as a businessman was hampered by his easy-come, easy-go attitude toward money. He once bought an even hundred head of hogs, tended them every day for a full year, and then sold the whole lot for exactly what he had paid for them. When Buck King pointed out that he hadn't made a cent on the investment, Bone countered that he knew he hadn't, but he did have free use of the stock for twelve months.[9]

Bone's court appearances also became popular stories. When some hogs were stolen from him, he located the animals two or three miles away from where they had been taken, and even though their marks had been changed he drove them back home. Taken into court by the person who had stolen the hogs in the first place, Bone was called to the stand and asked how long the marks had been changed. Hampered by his speech impediment and possibly a nip or two, Bone replied, "About a momph." "What's a momph?" the lawyer asked. "Why, a momph is firty days," answered Bone. "I thought everybody knew what a momph was."[10]

Bone once walked into a courtroom with his hat on and was promptly fined $20 by the judge. Bone calmly took two twenties out of his pocket, placed them on the table, and announced, "You better take forty, sir, 'cause I walked in here with my hat on, and I'm gonna walk out the same way."[11]

Will Addison, a resident of Okeechobee, recalled that Bone was once a witness in a cow-stealing case in Kissimmee. Bone had told someone that he had seen the cow in question and that she had a dewlap on her throat four feet long. In an attempt to identify the cow, the judge said to Bone, "Mr. Mizell, I understand that you said that cow had a dewlap on her four feet long." Bone hastily replied, "Judge, I was a-talkin' then, but I'm *a-swearin'* now."[12]

In fact, Bone was rarely intimidated by the law. Riding into Moore Haven after a prolonged cattle hunt in the swampland, he tied his horse to a palm tree in the town's small park, then lay down for a nap. Soon he was awakened by a policeman who told him he could not let his horse graze in the park, which the officer described as the pride of Moore Haven. "Well, that's all right," Bone said. "It won't hurt him. Besides, I'll be right here to watch him so he won't eat too much of it and take a drink and catch the swells." Bone then pulled a palm frond over his face and went back to sleep.[13]

When Les Dishong was sheriff of DeSoto County, he heard about a poker game going on at the Hollingsworth place, so he went out to investigate. He found Bone Mizell, Maury Hollingsworth, A. P. Hollingsworth, Zeb Parker, Russell King, and A. C. Williams sitting around the table with cards in hand. "Boys, I'm going to have to pull this game," the sheriff told the group. "But Sheriff," one of the players explained, "we're not playing for money—we're playing for poker chips." "They're the same as money," answered the sheriff. When the game broke up, Bone left with his pockets bulging with poker chips.

In Arcadia the next day the card players were fined $85 each. Bone waited until the others had paid off their fines, then sauntered up and counted out $85 in red, white, and blue chips. "Wait a minute," said the sheriff. "This ain't money." "You said it was yesterday," Bone reminded him as he turned and walked away.[14]

Bone loved to eat, and grits was one of his favorite foods. As Ziba King's foreman, he made a rule that if a cow hunter complained about the food served on roundups, he could not compete for the cash award offered by the boss for the largest number of calves branded. One morning at breakfast Bone remarked in a disgusted tone, "This dern grits is burned." Realizing that he was in danger of violating his own rule, he quickly added, "But that's the way I like it."[15]

After a hard day of cattle tending, the men looked forward to food and rest. Bone would often sing a song as they rode home:

The famed Arcadia House, meeting place of DeSoto County cattle-men. (Photo courtesy Lamar Lewis)

Headin' for the boarding house
Far, far away,
Oh how them boarders yell
When they hear the dinner bell,
Oh how them eggs do smell
Three times a day![16]

Bone was a frequent boarder at the Arcadia House, a popu-lar meeting place for DeSoto County cattlemen. One morning, having finished off a plate of grits topped with a quarter-pound of homemade butter, he ordered another helping of the same. His waitress became concerned about his eating so much high-priced butter. "Mr. Mizell, did you know that but-ter costs sixty-five cents a pound?" she asked. "Yes ma'am," replied Bone, "and wuff ever cent of it."[17]

Bone once accompanied Buck King on a business trip to New York, where they stayed at the famed Waldorf Astoria. The two arrived late at night and went straight to their hotel room. The next morning, as they walked along the sidewalk amid the city's scurrying crowds, Bone exclaimed, "My God, Buck! They must be having court week."[18]

Accustomed as he was to simpler fare, Bone understandably found the hotel's food service quite alien to him. Declining the menu since he couldn't read anyway, he advised Buck, "Just tell that fella to bring me some cucumbers and clabber."[19]

Back in Arcadia, Bone bought himself a new pair of brogans. Then he walked to the drugstore, purchased a bottle of castor oil, and poured it into the shoes to keep them from hurting his feet. While he was walking around town, someone asked him why the oil was sloshing out of his shoes. "That's the way I do it," answered Bone. "Some people put it on the outside and let it soak in. I put it on the inside and let it soak out."[20] In another version of this story Bone gave a different explanation: "Well, ordinarily I feel uncomfortable in town, but with my feet wet it's just like being at home."[21] Both versions are true to his character.

In Bone's time, a traveling show coming to town was an event sure to be attended by a large crowd, but the prankster cowboy often stole the limelight from the performers. When the circus came to Arcadia and set up next to the railroad tracks, he got into trouble for capturing the audience's atten-

The town of Arcadia, Florida, soon after its name was changed in 1886 from the less-dignified Tater Hill Bluff. (Florida Photographic Archives, Tallahassee)

tion and was escorted from the tent by circus officials. Once outside, Bone untied a tent rope and attached it to a freight train stopped nearby. As the train pulled out, it effectively took the circus with it. The next morning Bone was fined $75, but he didn't resent the penalty. He said the prank was worth an even thousand bucks to him—including $925 in personal satisfaction to see the show leave town the way it did.[22]

A confidence man came to town and set up a table at the county fair. Bone was present as he began hawking ten-dollar shares of stock in a company producing a new universal solvent. In glowing terms he described how the investment would make a fortune for shareholders within five years. Bone shouted from the rear of the crowd, "What's a universal solvent?" "Brother, I'm glad you asked that," the con man answered. "A universal solvent is a liquid that will dissolve anything it touches. Just think of all the uses such a product has." "Hold on there!" Bone interrupted. "What I want to know is what you're going to keep this universal solvent in when you get it made."[23]

With all the tricks he played on others, it is hardly surprising that Bone himself was often the target of practical jokes. Bay Johnson, son of Back Johnson, worked with Bone at the age of nineteen and recalled one such prank. One Fourth of July as he was riding with Bone and a group of cowboys beside the Hail cattle pens near Moore Haven, Bone was continually bothered by a foul smell. When they stopped, Bone opened one of his saddlebags and found a dead buzzard inside it. His fellow cowboys had a hearty laugh while Bone "muttered a few words to himself."[24]

Cy McClellan, another cowboy who worked with Bone, was known as a jester who would sometimes stretch the truth. Not wanting to be outdone, Bone remained alert for a challenge from him. One day, as the two were riding near Fort Ogden, Cy pointed across the vast ranges and pretended to identify a ship on the horizon. "Here comes the *Matador*," he said to Bone. "We been expecting her for some time now. Of course, she's pretty far out yet and I doubt if you can see her, mast and all." Bone studied the dry reaches to the west and replied, "Sure, I can see her, and there's a big horsefly on the mast."

"By gosh, you're right," Cy answered. "I just saw him blink his eye."[25]

Bone could not read the Bible, so he didn't consider it blasphemous to marry a couple with a Sears & Roebuck catalog.[26] He also conducted at least two funerals for cowboys who died out on the cattle ranges. But despite his reading handicap, Bone did know the Scriptures. When two men saw him one day under the influence of another kind of spirits, one of them remarked, "Why there's old Israel!" Somewhat agitated by the inconsiderate comment, Bone nevertheless had the last word: "I ain't Israel. I ain't Abraham, Isaac, or Jacob, but I'm Saul the son of Kish who went out seeking his father's asses, and I've found two of them!"[27]

Bone was also known to show his impish spirit in church. He went into a revival tent one Saturday night as the fervent worshippers were down on their knees praying. He either joined in or fell over them, ending up with his hand under a woman's dress. A couple of men nearby did not take the incident lightly and are said to have pommeled him "good and proper." Bone's only recourse was a blasphemous assault on his attackers.[28]

On another occasion Bone went to a camp meeting with a hangover from a drinking binge the night before. Hot, nauseated, and dehydrated, he couldn't keep his eyes off the water pitcher on the pulpit. He was the first one to the altar when the preacher called for those who needed prayer. Almost mad with thirst, Bone gulped huge draughts of water undetected by the preacher, who was devoutly praying for him.[29] In his condition, Bone needed both the water and the prayers.

One of Bone's relatives, Mrs. Zula Williams of Arcadia, was attending church services in Pine Level one Sunday when the cowboy showed up inebriated. Zula believed that Bone came specifically to have dinner with the congregation on the church grounds after the services. When they all stood up to sing, Bone held up his hymnal, but all he could sing was "chicken pie, chicken pie" over and over again, even long after the congregation had finished the hymn.[30]

One Sunday morning, after consuming quite a bit of moonshine, Bone rode up to a two-story church near Joshua Creek at meeting time. He went upstairs and talked with someone and was on his way back down when he slipped and fell head over heels to the bottom floor. Several people rushed to his aid. "Are you hurt?" one of them asked. "Naw," said Bone. "That's the way I always come downstairs."[31] He then mounted his horse and rode away, probably to get something more to drink.

7

"Drunk and disorderly"

"Nobody took Bone's drinking seriously, as he was better behaved while drunk than when sober and was everybody's friend when drinking."

Among the best-known stories told about Bone are those chronicling his drinking escapades. As is true of many Bone legends, some factual details behind these tales have been lost or revised, but their essential content is consistent with what is known of Bone's life and character, particularly his carefree and unconventional nature, his boisterous love of life, and his prankish spirit. These stories are still told around campfires and at rodeos.

If not the cause of his death, liquor certainly contributed to Bone's early demise—he was only fifty-eight when he died. But Bone loved to drink, and he was known to indulge in anything that had a kick, including, of course, the illegal whiskey readily available on the frontier. "Bayhead" moonshine was a rank, foul-tasting concoction; one drinker declared that "Florida liquor must be about four-thirds panther sweat."[1] Bone preferred the cheap but potent Jamaican rum; he also indulged in Cuban rum, known locally as augerdent from the slang expression "auger in," which meant becoming unconscious from drink.

One of Bone's drinking partners was cattleman James Newton Hollingsworth's son Mose, who was born in Pine Level in 1901. When Bone came into Arcadia and was unable to find whiskey, Mose and several other young men would buy grain alcohol for him at Jack Wey's drugstore. Together they would go out behind the store, cut the alcohol with grape juice, and drink while Bone regaled them with stories.[2]

Mayo Johnston, another contemporary of Bone's, recalled that the cowboy would drink anything containing alcohol when moonshine was unavailable. As a boy, Mayo and his family lived in the woods south of Fort Ogden. One day he and his mother, Dora, met Bone in the yard as he came riding up on his horse. Bone asked if there was anything in the house to drink. When Dora said no, he asked if she had any wood alcohol. "Yes," Dora replied. "But it'll kill you, Bone." "No, it won't kill me, Dora," he assured her. Apparently convinced, Dora brought the cowboy some wood alcohol. Bone placed a rag over the top of the container, strained a small portion of the lethal spirits into some water, and drank it.[3] Somehow it didn't kill him—at least that time.

Bone was known to drink anywhere under any conditions. As a young man barely out of his teens, Florida historian Donald B. McKay was well acquainted with Bone and at the time considered him a heroic figure. McKay was present the day Bone rode his horse into a Tampa saloon and took a drink at the bar while still sitting in the saddle. The saloon, owned by Pomp Gibson and formerly the residence of Judge Simon Turman, was situated on the northeast corner of what is now Lafayette and Ashley streets.[4]

Liquor could also be obtained as a remedy in drugstores. According to Lloyd Holton, a former DeSoto County sheriff, Bone once rushed into an Arcadia drugstore and told the druggist he needed a dose of liquor right away for a close friend who had been bitten by a rattlesnake. The druggist became excited and spilled some of the liquor on the counter. Shaking like a leaf, Bone scooped up the spilled liquor for himself, explaining to the druggist that "the damned snake had bitten him, too."[5]

Bone liked to sober up on lemon extract, which he was known to purchase at the combination store and post office in Bermont.

The proprietor, George W. Gatewood, also served as a Methodist minister; he had homesteaded in Bermont in 1907 and lived there until 1917.[6] On one of his trips for a few bottles of his special hangover medicine, Bone asked his friend if he had seen anything of a horse and buggy the previous evening. Bone explained that he had a little too much to drink the night before, and when he fell out of his buggy on the other side of a pond in front of the store, his horse went on but he couldn't. Later that day, some neighbors found the horse astride one of the buggy shafts. In the light carriage were Bone's pipe, tobacco, and burned fragments of one-dollar bills. When Gatewood asked the cowboy if he had been lighting his pipe with the money, Bone replied, "I guess so."[7]

Despite his fondness for liquor and his tendency to indulge whenever he could, Bone had some awareness of how alcohol affected him and was known to take certain precautions. Gatewood recalled that Bone, whom he considered strictly honest in his dealings, would not make a deal or sign a check while under the influence.[8] He would sometimes hire young Guy (Rattlesnake) Johnson to "ride herd" on him when he planned a drinking spree, "not that there was anything Johnson or anyone else could do if Bone should stampede."[9]

In one of the most popular Bone stories, told frequently by his friend Bob Whidden, the hard-drinking cowboy is the target of a practical joke in which he thought he was being resurrected from the dead. One night when drink got the best of Bone and he passed out, a group of cowboys carried him to an Arcadia graveyard and left him lying on one of the graves. One cowboy hid behind a nearby headstone to see how Bone would react when he came to. When he finally regained consciousness, Bone sat up, rubbed his eyes, and stared at his surroundings. In his folksy philosophical manner he commented, "Here it is Judgment Day, and I'm the first one up."[10]

Another widespread version of this story was recounted by V. K. Graham in the *Tampa Tribune*. Bone and other cowboys working for Ziba King often camped at a corral on part of the land at Cypress Bulks homesteaded by Graham's mother. Graham said that in an effort to discourage Bone's riding into town to get drunk, the other cowboys decided to scare some sense into him:

One night when he came to camp very drunk, he fell off his horse and lay passed out on the ground. The other cowboys placed his saddle under his head for a pillow and spread a horse blanket over him. Then they gathered a lot of dry cow chips and placed them in a circle around him—dry cow dung is very inflammable. The first one awake in the morning was to start the fires, give Bone's leg a twist to awaken him, and then lie down and pretend to be asleep. The plan worked perfectly. Bone stood up, gazed at the ring of fire, and uttered an oath and soliloquized, "Well, by ---! Dead and in hell! And I'm the first one up."[11]

Others say Bone raised himself up on one elbow, studied the flames for a moment, then announced: "Dead and gone to hell. No more 'n I expected."[12]

In the late 1950s, Florida author Wyatt Blassingame used the offices of the DeSoto Abstract Company in Arcadia to write a historical novel about the early cattle industry in DeSoto County. Using fictitious names for his characters, he wove into his novels some humorous incidents involving Bone Mizell, such as the story of his Judgment Day awakening in the cemetery. Blassingame also included another drinking story about the cowboy that is not so well known. One Saturday, Bone was hired to shovel manure from an Arcadia resident's barn and spread it on the garden. Bone disappeared before the job was finished, and several members of the family began looking for him. They checked the most logical hiding place: a makeshift corncrib in the back of the barn where a charred keg of sour mash was stored. But there was no sign Bone had even been there. It wasn't until Monday, when someone went to the crib to draw another jug of liquor for the house, that Bone—and the empty keg—were found. He had crawled under the building and used a brace and bit to bore a hole through the floor into the keg. Lying on his back, he would let the whiskey pour into his mouth, then plug the hole with his finger until he was ready for his next drink. When he passed out, the barrel emptied all over him as he lay immobile. It's a wonder he didn't drown.[13]

In another escapade, Bone and some friends had been cow

90

hunting in the pastures near La Belle on what was called the Northside when they decided to visit their Southside cronies. By the time the cowboys headed back to the Northside, they were full of liquor—and mischief. In their own boisterous manner of rejoicing and giving thanks for their friendship and entertainment, the noisy group sang "Praise God from whom all blessings flow" at the top of their lungs as they passed through La Belle. The town police promptly arrested Bone and his friends for disturbing the peace and placed them in the bullpen. In court the next morning, the mayor asked Bone if he had anything to say before a ten-dollar fine was imposed against him. "Judge," Bone replied, "I think La Belle or any other town is showing our constitutional and fundamental laws little respect when they deny the people the right to praise God on the public streets." Somewhat amused, yet impressed by the cowboy's sincerity, the mayor suspended the sentence on the promise of good behavior.[14]

A group of roustabouts in Arcadia once gave Bone a less-than-honorable sendoff when they discovered him passed out from liquor. They placed the unconscious cowboy inside a pine box used for shipping caskets, nailed it shut, addressed it to San Antonio, and put the box on the freight train. Bone came to somewhere up the line, and thinking he had been buried alive, he kicked, pounded, and hollered until someone released him.[15] (The same story has been told of a Kissimmee Valley cow hunter named Wilbur Shiever by Lawrence Silas, a respected black rancher who began his career as an employee of the Lykes brothers. Silas said that Shiever was the victim of this prank because he did something the other cowboys didn't like, and this was their way of getting rid of him.)[16]

Oddly enough, few stories are told about Bone and the opposite sex, and in most of these, he is once again under the influence. One cloudy day after he'd been drinking, he got lost riding in the woods near Kissimmee. Eventually he came to an unfamiliar house in a small clearing where he saw no one about except a woman. Worried he might frighten her in his condition, Bone tied himself securely to his saddle before approaching her. He assured the woman that he was harmless and merely wanted directions. After telling him how to find his way back, the woman stood in wonderment as Bone rode off.[17]

Bone never married, but he once applied for a marriage license, though he may not have been serious about it. Working in the courthouse at the time was young Martha Kreider, who waited on him. It was quail season and Clerk John H. Alford, Crawford Grey, and County Judge A. E. Pooser had taken the day off to go hunting. The judge had signed some marriage licenses in advance and instructed Martha that if anyone applied for one all she had to do was fill in the date and the names of the parties, affix the seal, and collect two dollars. The only other person in the courthouse with her was the tax collector, Myles Sauls, at the far end of the building. Hearing a hullabaloo outside, Martha peered out the window and saw Bone Mizell and Ed Gardner tying their horses to the hitching post. The two cowpokes stormed into the courthouse and began yelling and pounding on Judge Pooser's office door. Martha knew she had to investigate:

> The air was deep blue when I went out and asked what they wanted and told them the judge would not be in until Monday. I finally discovered Bone wanted a marriage license and I explained that I could give him one. Meanwhile his companion sauntered outside. Bone and I got down to business and all went well until I asked for the lady's name. He hesitated, then bellowed, "Ed, what in h--- was that woman's name?"
>
> By that time there was no doubt that he was roaring drunk. Ed was nowhere to be seen. When I said I could not give him the license without the fortunate young lady's name he started around the table toward me, and with another burst of blasphemy took after me.
>
> Grabbing the papers I started for the vault, but he was before me in the doorway. With one mighty heave I pushed the door shut, penning him inside. Then I ran for Myles and hid while he extricated Bone.[18]

Years later when someone sent Martha a clipping of Bone's obituary, she pondered over the disclosure that he had never married and considered she probably had something to do with that.[19] But it seems Bone was not cut out for the conventional life anyway. He once demonstrated what he thought of an orderly society with all its restrictions on his carefree way of life, and was promptly arrested on a charge of "drunk and disorderly and urinating on a public doorknob."[20] Doctor E. C. Aurin of Fort Ogden told Bessie Keene, Bone's grandniece, that the cowboy once rode into town "gloriously drunk" with dollar bills pinned all over his shirt. As he rode up and down the town streets, he let out an occasional cowboy yell as the dollar bills fluttered in the breeze.[21]

Not long before his death, the Kings sent Bone to dry out at a sanitarium in Hot Springs, Arkansas. He stayed off liquor for a while; then someone slipped him a bottle just before he boarded a train for home. In a short time he finished off the bottle and began running naked up and down the aisles of the passenger cars. Officials were forced to stop the train at a small town and have him locked up.[22]

To those who knew Bone well, it became obvious that his heavy drinking would eventually kill him, and Bone himself may have known when the end was near. He spent his last night in Joshua Creek at the home of his friend Leslie H. (Les) Avant. The next morning, July 14, 1921, Bone asked Avant to take him to town; on the way, he said that if something happened to him he wanted Avant to have his horse and saddle. From Arcadia, Bone took the train to Fort Ogden,[23] arriving at the village depot around eleven o'clock in the morning. From there he wired the Lykes brothers in Tampa for some money.

E. H. Morgan, the Fort Ogden agent for the Atlantic Coast Line Railway, was sick that day, so his son Robert was filling in for him. Bone sent his wire and sat down on a homemade couch in the ticket office. For a while he sat up but then stretched out on the couch. Morgan noticed Bone's face changing color and asked him to sit back up. As Bone did so he remarked, "Yeah, I'd better not lay down. I might die." These were the last words anyone heard Bone say. Before leaving for lunch at noon, Morgan asked Bone to sit on a bench in the waiting room, confident that the arms on the long seat would keep the ailing cowboy from lying down. He left him sitting on the bench, ate a hurried lunch, and returned im-

The Fort Ogden depot house, where Bone Mizell died in 1921. (Photo by the author)

mediately to find Bone lying dead on the floor.[24] "The money was received by wire, but Bone never received it," Morgan recalled. "He had died before its arrival, alone."[25]

Dr. Aurin was summoned to the depot. After what has been described as a casual glance, he pronounced Bone dead. Wondering about the hasty conclusion, a fellow known as Squeaky asked the doctor, "How do you know? You ain't tested him." "I don't need to test him," the doctor said. "I know that right now Old Bone would test a good 90 proof."[26]

After the pronouncement, another local resident, Wylie (Cryin') Miller, kept following the doctor around and asking what killed Bone. In exasperation Dr. Aurin finally told the persistent Miller the reason Bone died was that his heart stopped beating. Believing he alone had the inside story, Miller scurried around town spreading the word that he knew what caused the cowboy's death. When asked what killed Bone, Miller would proudly announce, "Why—his heart stopped."[27]

The sole signatory of the death certificate for the "cow

hunter" was L. L. Morgan, an undertaker and brother of the depot agent. Entered as the cause of death is the brief but explicit postmortem, "Moonshine—went to sleep and did not wake up."[28]

Bone's funeral was held in Arcadia the next day at the home of his nephew Jesse B. Mizell, Jr., with the Reverend J. H. Derrberry officiating. Florida's most celebrated cowboy was buried in the Joshua Creek Cemetery. The pallbearers were Hooker Parker, W. H. Seward, J. M. Alderman, Leonard Smith, Henry Avant, and Paul Spear, all close friends of the deceased.[29]

8

"The crowning stunt
of Bone Mizell's life"

"And so somewhere, an old Florida cracker lies in a stately grave
he never dreamed of, and a disillusioned boy sleeps in the loneli-
ness he wanted to find."

Bone Mizell's most outlandish and best-remem-
bered prank was his deliberate substitution of the remains of a
friend for those of another man, which he shipped by train to
New Orleans for reinterment at the request of the other man's
family. This bizarre incident, originally circulated among
Florida's cow camps, has become legendary. As is generally true
of folktales, versions of the story have become garbled over the
years, including the identities of those involved. But the incident
actually happened, and certain details are substantiated in various published accounts. Some of these identify Bone Mizell and
his friend John Underhill by name, while the unfortunate
stranger, who still lies in an unmarked grave in the Florida
rangeland, is referred to as a rich Jew from New Orleans.

The individual most familiar with the facts of the corpse-
switching was probably Frank H. Stout, editor of the *Fort Myers
Press*, who heard the story from Bone himself on November 7,
1893. It is unfortunate that Stout did not record everything
Bone told him about the incident, for he undoubtedly obtained

certain facts that have been lost in the oral tradition. Stout published this account of his visit with Bone:

> Mr. Bone Mizell, of Arcadia, called on us Tuesday evening. In the course of conversation—Bone doing the talking—we learned of the final disposition of the remains of old John Underhill. We would like to see the story in print, as Bone tells it; but still no writer could give his inimitable style, and the curious narrative would lose much of its point. At any rate, poor John Underhill rests under a $3,000 monument in New Orleans, and the rich Jew's remains lie planted near Punta Gorda, his only monument the saw palmetto; and the festive tumblebug sings his last, sad requiem. Bone is a plumb good one, and may he long live to cheer his fellow man through this life.[1]

Florida historian Albert DeVane lived his entire life in Bone Mizell country. He considered the story of John Underhill's "delayed death journey to New Orleans" the greatest of all tales told about Bone. However, in his account of the incident, John Underhill is given the middle name Matthew, which was actually the name of John's youngest brother.[2]

Miami newspaperman Stephen Trumbull obtained particulars of the strange event from Bone's friend and one-time employer Buck King and from Sanford D. Blazer, a salesman for the Welles Crating Company in Nocatee, both of whom had heard the story from Bone himself. Trumbull called the story the pièce de résistance in a long list of Mizell legends.[3] He later wrote about the tale under the titles "Bone and the Transposed Bodies" and "That Old Cracker Finally Got His Train Ride."[4]

Despite the extensive files of the Underhill family genealogist, relatively little is known of Bone's friend John Underhill, who lived as an elusive pioneer on the remote Florida frontier. He was born in 1823, the son of Joseph Underhill and the former Nancy Hilliard. He had three brothers: Thomas, William, and Matthew. Between 1862 and 1877, John's father, a veteran of the War of 1812, appears in the Polk County tax lists, but by 1880 he resided in Pine Level, Manatee County.[5]

John Underhill married Keziah Tucker in Hillsborough County on September 11, 1854.[6] When the Seminole War of

1856 broke out, John was mustered into William B. Hooker's company as a corporal and fought Indians along the Peace River and in the Everglades.[7] He and his three brothers served in the Confederate army during the Civil War. John was a member of Roll Company E, Seventh Florida Infantry, known locally as the South Florida Bulldogs.[8] William and Matthew served in Munnerlyn's Cattle Guard Battalion; Thomas, a Confederate leader in the Peace River area, was killed by Union troops in 1864.[9]

On March 28, 1876, John married Sophia Savage (née Thompson) in Manatee County;[10] the fate of his first wife is unknown. John and Sophia Underhill and four children appear in the 1880 U.S. Census for Manatee County. In the 1885 state census, John Underhill, age sixty-two, his wife, Sophia, and three children are listed as residents of the portion of Monroe County exclusive of the island of Key West. (Until 1887 Monroe County stretched from the Caloosahatchee River south to Key West.) Soon thereafter, John died in the cattle country near Lee Branch north of Punta Gorda. The 1900 U.S. Census lists Sophia Underhill, a daughter, and a stepson as residents of Sanibel Island across San Carlos Bay from the cattle port of Punta Rassa.[11]

Sometime between 1885 and 1893, Bone received word that his old friend John was near death in a cow camp near Lee Branch, so he rode to the camp to take care of him. Several days after his arrival, John died and Bone took charge of the funeral arrangements. On his return from picking out a burial site, he found that some of the cow hunters were preparing to bathe the body before dressing it in store-bought clothes. Bone admonished the well-intended group: "Hellfire no, you ain't going to wash him. You all know he'd never allow it if he was alive and you all ain't going to take advantage of him now he's dead."[12] So they buried John as he was in a solitary grave out on the range. Research conducted in 1943 by Arcadia high school students, who obtained details from their parents and grandparents for their early history of DeSoto County, confirms this story of John's burial.[13]

After John's death, a young Jewish boy drifted into the cattle country and, oddly enough, teamed up with Bone. Legend has it that the youth was broken in health and disillusioned after years of travel throughout the world. Eventually the boy died out on the cattle ranges after a long dry spell, which prevented Bone from hauling the body by flatboat over the normally flooded prairies. Bone and his fellow cowboys decided to bury the corpse next to John Underhill's grave.

A few years passed before the youth's wealthy parents, who lived in New Orleans, learned of the death of their son and discovered a few particulars about his burial. They immediately sent money to a local undertaker to have the body exhumed and returned home for reinterment in the family plot. When the rains came, the undertaker paid Bone to retrieve the body. Helping Bone was Joe Daughtrey, the son of a Bradenton cattleman.

Bone later confessed to friends that he took the money under false pretenses and never did send home the youth's remains. He claimed the scheme was his idea alone, and he did not want Joe to be held responsible. Moreover, Bone consistently maintained he was guilty of no wrongdoing. He explained that on the ride out to the two unmarked graves, two things were on his mind. First, he knew that the youth was fed up with everything, most of all with traveling. He had made it clear to Bone that he never wanted to see another railroad train and never wanted to go back home. Second, Bone's friend John had always yearned to take a train ride and never had enough money to do so. "Well, sir, it didn't seem right," Bone confided. "It seemed even less right after a few drinks to sort of fortify us for the digging job. Here was a free train ride ahead, a funeral so damned fine this country had never even seen the likes of it—probably with four white horses pulling the hearse."[14] So it was that upon arriving at the burial site Bone pointed out the old cracker's grave as that of the young Jew and told his helpers to dig, figuring that John's reposing in a costly tomb would be a measure of justice.[15]

As the Underhill–Jewish boy story was passed on through the years, the identity of the "old cracker who finally got his train ride" was often changed in deference to living family members or because the true name was seldom communicated and was therefore soon forgotten; Underhill's aliases include Bill Redd,[16] Zipe Hendrix,[17] Old Man Woodruff,[18] Old Man Smith,[19] Ol' Sheiver,[20] and Jughead Something-or-other.[21] Meanwhile, the name of the out-of-state visitor to Florida's cattle country, whose remains still repose in an unmarked grave, appears to be lost. The young Jew from New Orleans has been given various epithets in print, including "a young Philadelphia consumptive,"[22] "an unpopular English remittance man,"[23] "a young scapegrace from Vermont,"[24] and "a young Northern runaway."[25]

There is a sequel to Bone's "crowning stunt," known only to a few people outside the Mizell family. Bone's grave in the Joshua Creek Cemetery remained unmarked for over thirty years before some of his friends decided to donate a tombstone for his final resting place. As fate would have it, the small inscribed marker was placed on the wrong grave. One night kinsmen Mayo and Smoot Johnston discreetly moved the headstone to its rightful place.[26] No doubt Bone himself would have chuckled over this ironic turn of events.

9

"Ballad of Bone Mizelle"

"In Mrs. Ruby Carson's rhymed version, first published in The Florida Teacher, *Old Man Woodruff-Underhill becomes Bill Redd, the
scene Pine Island and the dead stranger a native of Vermont."*

■■■■■■ The story of Bone's corpse-swapping prank
spread throughout the peninsular cow country. The incident
was a favorite topic of gossip in Kissimmee, a frontier cattle
town that catered to cow hunters. A. E. Bearden ran the Kentuck
Exchange, a drinking establishment with a ride-up window of-
fering streetside service to cowboys who chose not to dismount.
A large sign over the building advertised "Wines, Liquors, Schlitz
Milwaukee Beer, etc.," though one resident claimed there was always plenty to drink without the "etc.," whatever that included.[1]
The wide and spacious Broadway, lined with boardwalks and
running through the center of town, was said to be the only
grass-covered main street in the United States. Grazing cattle
kept the Bermuda grass closely cropped, and the animals slept
on the turf at night, much to the discomfiture of wayfarers.[2]
Bone himself rode into town quite often, no doubt enhancing his
reputation with each visit, and the locals loved to regale listeners
with stories of the celebrated cowboy.

Over time, names of characters, locales, and other details

were changed in various accounts of the swap. One version of the story that circulated around Kissimmee sets the action in Osceola County. It was said that a Yankee had lived in Kissimmee for several years prior to his death. Bone agreed to take on the job of digging up the Yankee's remains and shipping them north at his family's request. Instead, however, Bone purposely dug up and shipped the remains of a local resident named Sheiver, who had never traveled beyond his own county.[3]

From the same locale emerged a completely revamped account of the substituted corpse. Bone does not appear at all in this version of the story. The two main characters are a wealthy man from Detroit, who came to Florida for a fishing trip on the Kissimmee River, and a native cracker known as Old Bill, who had always yearned to travel but never saw the sights of the world. The wealthy fisherman is said to have died from an infection he contracted on a trip downstream. With no means of preserving the corpse, his guide was forced to bury him in a small

The grass-covered main street of Kissimmee, Florida, about 1895. On the left is the Pat Allen building, behind which stands the Tropical Hotel. On the right is the original State Bank of Kissimmee. (Photo courtesy Sam L. Lupfer)

clearing beside the river where Old Bill had been buried a few years earlier. Sometime later, at the request of the visitor's widow, a body was shipped back to Detroit. Unbeknownst to the widow, she received the remains of Old Bill, and she wrote a gracious thank-you letter to the guide. She sent along a lengthy obituary from a Detroit newspaper describing her deceased husband's memorial service, which was attended by a number of prominent citizens, including the mayor. Proud of what he had done, the guide figured Old Bill was grateful, too.[4]

It was in the Kissimmee area that Ruby Leach Carson heard the story of Bone's most famous prank and immortalized both man and deed in a poem which became the lyrics of a song. Some of the details in the lyrics, which are reprinted here with music, reflect the various versions of the story that have been circulated. But factual inconsistencies aside, "Ballad of Bone Mizelle," as Ms. Carson's poem was titled, stands as a meaningful and lasting tribute to this frontier folk hero.

Ruby Leach Carson was born on June 9, 1894, in Joplin, Missouri, where she attended public school. Her father, John Leach, was a mining engineer. In 1910 Ruby taught school in a remote rural area in Texas, but she found the "uncouth" West of those days distasteful and inappropriate for a young girl of sixteen.[5] The Leach family moved to Dade County, Florida, in 1915. Her father took up farming while Ruby joined the staff of the *Miami Daily Metropolis* as a reporter, covering local and distant assignments for a national news service in the western states and Mexico. On one occasion, she had to disguise herself in flashy clothes and a wig to cover a story on unlawful activities in Miami. As a reporter, she also took part in a treasure hunt in Central America.

In 1923, Ruby founded the *Homestead Leader* in Dade County with her sister and brother-in-law. Three years later, she married James M. Carson, a Miami lawyer and member of a pioneer Kissimmee family. The couple bought a place in Osceola County on the south side of Lake Marian near Kenansville, where Ruby heard stories of the legendary Bone Mizell and gathered material for some of her articles on Florida history, much of which she gleaned from conversations and interviews with local residents. An observant and careful researcher, she "wel-

☆

BALLAD OF BONE MIZELLE

At Kissimmee they tell of old M. Bone Mizelle
  And the stranger who died on his hands;
How he died in dry season, and that was the reason
  He was buried awhile on Bone's lands.

He was buried awhile on that pine and palm isle
  In a swamp under Florida's sun
By the Cracker who nursed him, who loved him and cursed him
  Just before his demise had begun.

"Jes take this news ka'mly," Bone wrote to the family
  The deceased had left livin' up north,
"I can send th' remains when there come up some rains
  And us pine island folk can go forth.

"So providin' yuh ask it, I'll dig up th' casket" . . .
  Which was done when the season brought rain,
And the river could float the flat-bottomed boat
  And the dead boy could travel again.

When Bone went with the coffin, he smiled much too of'en
  On the boat and en route to the car.
At the train he said "Gimme one fare from Kissimmee
  To Vermont! Ain't this corpse goin' far!"

Thus the money was spent that the family had sent
  And a friend of Bone's said the next day:
"So yuh shipped that lad hum?" And Bone said: "No, by gum—
  For I thought hit all over this way:

"As his kinfolks air strangers to all of us rangers,
  Why not give some dead Cracker this ride?
Why not make all this fuss over some pore ole cuss
  Who in life hadn't wallered in pride?

"So instead of that Yank with his money and rank
  Who had been 'round and seen lots of fun,
I jes' dug up Bill Redd and I sent him instead
  For ole Bill hadn't traveled 'round none."

Original printing of the "Ballad of Bone Mizelle" (The Florida Teacher,
February-March 1939).

comed the opportunity to meet and talk with pioneers from whom she gained valuable information for her studies, which featured fact rather than fiction."[6] Among her literary works are *Fabulous Florida*, a fourth-grade textbook, and *Florida from Indian Trail to Space Age*, a comprehensive three-volume history that she coauthored with Charlton Tebeau, the noted historian from the University of Miami.

As a poet, Ms. Carson won considerable acclaim for her wide variety of both serious and light verse. Her levity is demonstrated in the following quatrain she wrote for her young son and daughter:

> I'm not so unkind, but to my mind
>   Whoever first served spinach,
> Should meet some late, but awful fate,
>   Like whooping cough or skin itch.[7]

The characteristic internal rhyme within the first and third lines of her quatrains, along with the conventional end rhyme

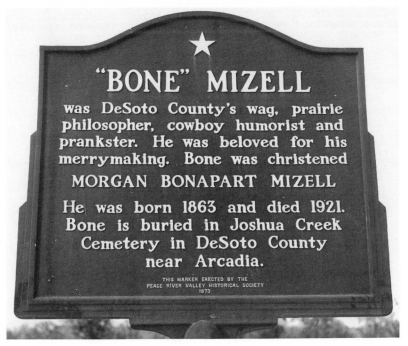

Historical marker to Bone Mizell, dedicated March 10, 1974, in Pioneer Park, Zolfo Springs, Florida.

Ruby Leach Carson (1884–1977), photographed about the time she wrote her poetic tribute to Bone Mizell. (Photo courtesy Dr. Carol Sanford)

The Ballad of Bone Mizell

Original
poem by
Ruby Leach Carson

Music by
Dottie and
Jim Bob Tinsley

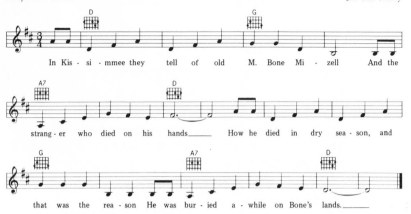

In Kis - si - mmee they tell of old M. Bone Mi - zell And the strang - er who died on his hands_____ How he died in dry sea - son, and that was the rea - son He was bur - ied a - while on Bone's lands._____

1. In Kissimmee they tell of old M. Bone Mizell
   And the stranger who died on his hands;
   How he died in dry season, and that was the reason
   He was buried awhile on Bone's lands.

2. He was buried awhile on a palm and pine isle
   In a swamp under Florida's sun
   By the cowboy who nursed him, who loved him and cursed him
   Just before his demise had begun.

3. "Jus' take the news ka'mly," Bone wrote to the family
   The deceased had left living up North.
   "I can send th' remains when we start to have rains
   And us Pine Island folks can go forth.

4. "So, providin' you ask it, I'll dig up the casket."
   Which he did when the season brought rain.
   And the river could float an old flat-bottomed boat
   And the dead boy could travel again.

5. While moving the coffin, Bone smiled much too of'en
   On the boat while en route to the car.
   At the train he said, "Gimme one fare from Kissimmee
   To Vermont. Ain't this corpse goin' far!"

6. So the money was spent that the family had sent,
   And a Friend asked old Bone the next day:
   "So you shipped the lad, hum?" Bone replied, "No, by gum—
   For I thought it all over this way:

7. "As his kinfolks are strangers to all of us rangers,
   I will give some dead Cracker this ride.
   Why not make all th' fuss over some pore old cuss
   Who in life hadn't wallered in pride?

8. "So, instead of the Yank with his money and rank
   Who'd been 'round and seen lots of fun,
   I jus' dug up Bill Redd and I sent his instead,
   For ole Bill hadn't traveled 'round none."

of the second and fourth lines, ensures a melodic and rhythmic structure that allows her poems to be translated effectively into song lyrics. This is particularly true of her widely printed poem about Bone Mizell. "Ballad of Bone Mizelle" first appeared in the February–March 1939 issue of *The Florida Teacher* on a regular poetry page edited by Vivian Yeiser Laramore, poet laureate of Florida. The work was reprinted by the Laramore-Rader Poetry Group in an anthology of Florida verse in 1964.[8]

Bone's folk-hero status was again formally recognized when the Peace River Historical Society erected a historical marker to him at the Pioneer Museum in Zolfo Springs on March 10, 1974. The dedication and memorial services were attended by a number of dignitaries, historians, folklorists, friends, and relatives. At the dedication, Geraldine Kent Thrailkill of Wauchula offered another poetic tribute to Bone in a composition recalling his most famous adventures.

The Bone Mizell Story

The pearl in Florida's night cast a warm glow
O'er towns and prairies Bone Mizell used to know;
The hard-riding, fun-loving cowboy of long ago
Who once marked a "mean critter" with his teeth in one throw.

In Bone's day "law" was a word few reckoned with at all.
Rustlers stole cattle from the range or from a stall;
Cowboys would race into town eager for a brawl
Hell-bent on a fight for reasons they could not recall.

A cold-eyed marshal charged Bone with breaking the law
When he roped and branded a couple of strays he saw
In the woods with little to graze on but pinestraw.
Though hauled into court, not a day in jail did Bone draw!

Wild rebel yells hailed the verdict, which made the Judge frown.
Bone rode his horse right up to the bar in old Tampa town

And demanded drinks for friends who had not let him
  down,
They bribed the jury with food, rum and Have-a-Tampas
  brown.

To this day when cowpokes have rid their beds of
  pinecone
Near a smouldering campfire beyond which mosquitos
  drone,
Panthers scream, owls hoot and nervous cows low and
  moan,
They will bring to mind stories of old cowboy Bone.

The time Bone awoke in the graveyard and thought 'twas
  Judgment Day
And 'lowed as how he was the "fust ter rise" and had not
  time to pray,
Unaware he'd been put there during a nightlong
  drinking fray;
His pranksters knew that within a week Bone would make
  them pay.

Amid guffaws they will recall Bone's friend from Yankee
  land,
A youth whose life was short and Bone buried him in
  Florida sand,
While the body of a cracker who'd never had a train ride
  grand
He shipped to the boy's family and they interred it like
  Bone planned!

Ere the stars fade they'll repeat the parson's episode;
As he walked and prayed, the Reverend spied scorched
  money by the road,
Hard-by stood Bone's buggy, minus horse to pull the load
And proof he's lit cigars with dollar bills in his night's
  abode.

In a railway station Bone heeded a mute command
To search for greener pastures on a far-away strand;

Sans adieu he boarded a train for the Promised Land
And there Bone greets old friends with jokes and welcom-
   ing hand.[9]

In the dedication speech, Bill Bevis, chairman of the Florida Public Service Commission, called Bone "the most colorful, hardest working, and hardest playing cowboy the state
has ever known."[10] A few years earlier, Bone's hometown
newspaper had aptly described him as "a big, loose, laughing
fellow who turned the sights and sounds of the prairies into
stories."[11] It is these stories that keep alive the memory of this
remarkable cowboy whose life mirrored an era marked indeli-
bly with his spirit.

notes

Chapter 1

Note: Chapter title from George Leposky, "Bone Mizell: Cracker Cowboy," *Florida Magazine, Sentinel Star* (Orlando), May 20, 1973, p. 20; epigraph from Albert DeVane, "Napoleon Bonaparte (Bone) Mizell Loved to Watch Bobcats Fighting," *Tampa* (Fla.) *Tribune,* December 28, 1958, p. 6D.

1. Jabbo Gordon, "Bone Mizelle—In the 1890's, He Was DeSoto's Wildest Cowboy," *Arcadian* (Arcadia, Fla.), June 17, 1976, pp. 7C–9C.

2. John Bartholf, "An Early Pine Level Postmaster Reflects on the Occasion of America's First 100 Years," *Arcadian* (Arcadia, Fla.), June 17, 1976, p. 10C.

3. Deed Book E, Manatee County, Clerk of Circuit Court Office, Bradenton, Florida, filed January 13, 1883, p. 125; Deed Book K, filed January 3, 1887, pp. 741–42.

4. Interview with Mrs. Manila Coates (age eighty), May 24, 1978, Bradenton, Florida.

5. DeVane, "Napoleon Bonaparte (Bone) Mizell Loved to Watch Bobcats Fighting."

6. Nixon Smiley, "Bone Mizelle: Will Rogers of the Cattle Rustlers," *Miami* (Fla.) *Herald,* August 20, 1967, p. 10C.

7. Ibid.

8. Joe A. Akerman, Jr., *Florida Cowman, a History of Florida Cattle Raising* (Kissimmee: Florida Cattlemen's Association, 1976), pp. 186–87.

9. Margaret Roesch, "'Real Old-Timer' Relates Interesting Railroad Incidents," *Tampa* (Fla.) *Tribune,* December 3, 1950, p. 13C.

10. Gene Burnett, "Florida's Hard-Drinking Cattle Thief of a Cowboy Hero," *Florida Trend*, May 1976, pp. 96–98.

11. *Miscellaneous Records 1*, DeSoto County, Clerk of Circuit Court Office, Arcadia, Florida, pp. 252–53.

12. "Cattle Raising in South Florida," *Florida Times-Union and Citizen* (Jacksonville), December 19, 1897, sec. 5, p. 40.

13. Margaret Roesch, "More Details of the Mizell Family," *Tampa* (Fla.) *Tribune*, December 14, 1952, p. 6C.

14. Jennie A. Reninger, "Cowhand Gives $9,000 Party," *Atlanta* (Ga.) *Journal Magazine*, March 13, 1932, p. 7.

15. Interview with H. Logan King, Jr. (Ziba King's grandson), April 20, 1979, Lutz, Florida.

16. Jack Beater, *Tales of South Florida and the Ten Thousand Islands* (Fort Myers: Ace Press, 1965), pp. 110-12.

17. Roesch, "'Real Old-Timer' Relates Interesting Railroad Incidents."

18. Reninger, "Cowhand Gives $9,000 Party."

Chapter 2

Note: Chapter title from Ora Mizell, "History of Prominent Mizell Family Recorded," *Tampa* (Fla.) *Tribune*, August 16, 1953, p. 4C; epigraph from Allen R. Taylor, "The First Sheriff of Orange County, Florida," manuscript, Orlando, Florida, October 1975, p. 4.

1. Folks Huxford, *Pioneers of Wiregrass Georgia*, 3 vols. (Jacksonville: Cooper Press, 1957), 3: 210–11.

2. "Some Camden County Officers," *Georgia Genealogical Magazine* 8 (April 1963): 485–92.

3. Huxford, *Pioneers of Wiregrass Georgia*.

4. Fifth Census of the United States, 1830, Population Schedules, Territory of Florida, Alachua County, microcopy no. 19, roll no. 15, p. 5, National Archives, Washington, D.C.

5. Ancient Records 1826–48 [Book B Deeds], Alachua County, Clerk of Circuit Court Office, Gainesville, Florida, pp. 46–47.

6. "More Indian Murders," *Florida Herald and Southern Democrat* (St. Augustine), November 29, 1838, p. 2.

7. Taylor, "The First Sheriff of Orange County, Florida."

8. Huxford, *Pioneers of Wiregrass Georgia*.

9. Deed Record A, Alachua County, Clerk of Circuit Court Office, Gainesville, Florida, p. 195.

10. Seventh Census of the United States, 1850, Population Schedules, Territory of Florida, Alachua County, pp. 2–3; Benton County, p. 23.

11. Deed Record D, Alachua County, Clerk of Circuit Court Office, Gainesville, Florida, pp. 64, 83–84.

12. T. Frederick Davis, "Florida's Part in the War with Mexico," *Florida Historical Quarterly* 20 (January 1942): 253–59.

13. "Enoch Everett Mizell, 1806–1887," *South Florida Pioneers* 3 (January 1975): 13–17.

14. Board of State Institutions, *Soldiers of Florida in the Seminole Indian–Civil and Spanish-American Wars* (Live Oak: Democrat Book and Job Print, 1903), pp. 16, 19–22.

15. Taylor, "The First Sheriff of Orange County, Florida."

16. William Fremont Blackman, *History of Orange County, Florida* (De Land: E. O. Painter Printing Co., 1927), pp. 87, 167.

17. Dora McLenon Johnston, "Additional History of the Lake Okeechobee Country," manuscript, North Fort Myers, Florida, July 1965, pp. 5–9.

18. "Memoirs of Dora McLenon Johnston," manuscript, North Fort Myers, Florida, November 18, 1952–April 9, 1961, pp. 18–19.

Chapter 3

Note: Chapter title from Kyle S. Van Landingham, "Early History of the Kissimmee River Valley," *South Florida Pioneers* 7 (January 1976): 3–5; epigraph from Allen R. Taylor, "The First Sheriff of Orange County, Florida," manuscript, Orlando, Florida, October 1975, p. 6.

1. "Murdered," *Florida Peninsular* (Tampa), March 16, 1870, p. 2.

2. T. C. Bridges, *Florida to Fleet Street* (London: Hutchinson & Co., 1926), p. 39.

3. Gene Barber, "Moses Barber," *Magnolia Monthly* 3 (November 1965): 16–18.

4. Nixon Smiley, "Civil War Sparked Bitter Cattle Feud," *Miami* (Fla.) *Herald*, October 20, 1968, p. 6F.

5. Barber, "Moses Barber."

6. Myrtle Hilliard Crow, "Basses Tamed Wild Country," *Osceola Sun* (Kissimmee, Fla.), October 23, 1972, p. 2.

7. Interview with Tom J. Bumby, December 29, 1978, Tavares, Florida.

8. Board of State Institutions, *Soldiers of Florida in the Seminole Indian–Civil and Spanish-American Wars* (Live Oak: Democrat Book and Job Print, 1903), pp. 181–84, 202–5.

9. Company Muster Roll, Lesley's Mtd. Vols. (6 Months, 1857–58), Florida (Seminole War), National Archives and Records Service, Washington, D.C.

10. Board of State Institutions, *Soldiers of Florida*, pp. 199–200.

11. Taylor, "The First Sheriff of Orange County, Florida," pp. 4–5.

12. Board of State Institutions, *Soldiers of Florida*, pp. 179-80.

13. W. R. O'Neal, "Memoirs of a Pioneer," *Sentinel Star* (Orlando, Fla.), March 9, 1941, p. 6.

14. Eve Bacon, *Orlando, a Centennial History* (Chuluota: Mickler House, 1975), pp. 29–32.

15. Smiley, "Civil War Sparked Bitter Cattle Feud."

16. Gene Barber, "The Barber-Mizell Feud," manuscript, Macclenny, Florida, 1964, p. 3.

17. "Circuit Court Volusia County," *Florida Union* (Jacksonville), November 4, 1868, p. 2.

18. Bacon, *Orlando, a Centennial History.*

19. Minute Book A, April 20, 1847–January 30, 1883, Orange County, Clerk of Circuit Court Office, Orlando, Florida, pp. 265–66, 274, 276.

20. Ibid., pp. 294–95.

21. Ibid., pp. 293, 295–96.

22. Indictment for forcibly confining and imprisoning another against his will, *The State of Florida v. Moses E. Barber and Moses B. F. Barber*, spring term 1869, Microfilm Dept., Clerk of Circuit Court, Orlando, Florida.

23. Minute Book A, p. 314.

24. Evidence of George Bass, *The State of Florida v. Moses E. Barber/ Moses B. F. Barber/Thomas Johnson*, filed July 20, 1869, A. H. Stockton, Clerk, Microfilm Dept., Clerk of Circuit Court, Orlando, Florida.

25. Ibid.

26. Indictment for forcibly confining a person against his will, *The State of Florida v. Moses E. Barber/Moses B. F. Barber/Thomas Johnson*, no. 25, filed July 26, 1869, A. H. Stockton, Clerk, Microfilm Dept., Clerk of Circuit Court, Orlando, Florida.

27. Minute Book A, pp. 320, 325.

28. Evidence of David W. Mizell, *The State of Florida v. Moses E. Barber/Moses B. F. Barber/Thomas Johnson*, filed July 16, 1869, A. H. Stockton, Clerk, Microfilm Dept., Clerk of Circuit Court, Orlando, Florida.

29. Barber, "The Barber-Mizell Feud."

30. Eve Bacon, "Orange County's First Pioneer Lies Buried in Orlando's Newest Park," *Florida Magazine, Sentinel Star* (Orlando), January 19, 1969, pp. 8F–9F.

31. Ibid.

32. Nixon Smiley, "Blood Feud at Canoe Creek," *Sunday Magazine, Miami* (Fla.) *Herald*, April 16, 1967, pp. 8–9.

33. Ibid.

34. *Florida Peninsular* (Tampa), April 13, 1870, p. 2.

35. U.S. Census Office, Ninth Census, 1870 [Census of Florida], Original Census Schedules, Schedule 2, Persons who died during the year ending 1st June 1870, Alachua-Washington, microcopy no. 87-AA, reel 3, pp. 5, 72.

36. *Florida Peninsular* (Tampa), April 13, 1870, p. 2.

37. "The War Goes Bravely on in Orange County," *Florida Peninsular* (Tampa), May 25, 1870, p. 2.

38. Board of County Commissioners 1, 1869–79, Orange County, Clerk of Circuit Court Office, Orlando, Florida, pp. 46–48.

39. Indictment for murder, *The State of Florida v. Moses E. Barber,* Circuit Court for the 7th Judicial District, Orange County, no. 241, filed November 11, 1870, Microfilm Dept., Clerk of Circuit Court, Orlando, Florida.

40. Gene Barber, "The Mystery of Moses Barber," *Magnolia Monthly* 3 (November 1965): 19.

41. Barber, "The Barber-Mizell Feud."

42. Application for Letters of Administration on the Estate of Moses E. Barber, Case No. 44, Columbia County, Offices of Clerks of Court, Lake City, Florida, filed December 24, 1870. Also Order Book A2, p. 7.

43. Barber, "Moses Barber."

44. Quinn Bass, Receiver in the Case of Rebecca E. Barber, Administratrix of Moses E. Barber, deceased, against Robert Bullock and James H. Howard, Minute Book A, pp. 331, 333.

45. *Early Settlers of Orange County, Florida* (Orlando: C. E. Howard, 1915), p. 55.

46. "A. J. Barber Died at Ripe Old Age," *Evening Reporter-Star* (Orlando, Fla.), August 21, 1916, p. 1.

47. Bridges, *Florida to Fleet Street*, pp. 83–84.

48. "Pompano Is Now Incorporated Town," *Miami* (Fla.) *Daily Metropolis,* June 8, 1908, p. 1.

49. "Judge Mizell, G.O.P. Leader, Died Yesterday," *Miami* (Fla.) *Daily Metropolis,* November 10, 1913, p. 1.

Chapter 4

Note: Chapter title from Gene Burnett, "Florida's Hard-Drinking Cattle Thief of a Cowboy Hero," *Florida Trend,* May 1976, p. 96; epigraph from George Leposky, "Bone Mizell: Cracker Cowboy," *Florida Magazine, Sentinel Star* (Orlando), May 20, 1973, p. 20.

1. A. H. Curtiss, "Punta Rassa and the Cattle Trade," *Bartow* (Fla.) *Informant,* November 24, 1883, p. 1.

2. Deed Book K, Manatee County, Clerk of Circuit Court Office, Bradenton, Florida, pp. 742–44.

3. *Fort Ogden* (Fla.) *News,* February 25, 1887, p. 3.

4. Albert DeVane and Park DeVane, *DeVane's Early Florida History* (Sebring: Sebring Historical Society, 1978), pp. 305–8.

5. Deed Book G, Manatee County, Clerk of Circuit Court Office, Bradenton, Florida, recorded January 12, 1886, p. 937; Deed Book H, recorded February 16, 1886, p. 301.

6. Deed Record 14, DeSoto County, Clerk of Circuit Court Office, Arcadia, Florida, filed July 30, 1889, pp. 93–94; Deed Record 22, filed November 7, 1891, pp. 57–58.

7. Marks & Brands 1, DeSoto County, Clerk of Circuit Court Office, Arcadia, Florida, pp. 11–12, 15, 21, 50, 58.

8. Miscellaneous Records 1, DeSoto County, Clerk of Circuit Court Office, Arcadia, Florida, pp. 186–87, 192–93, 241–42, 252–53.

9. Jennie A. Reninger, "Cowhand Gives $9,000 Party," *Atlanta* (Ga.) *Journal Magazine,* March 13, 1932, p. 7.

10. George W. Gatewood, *On Florida's Coconut Coasts* (Punta Gorda: *Punta Gorda Herald,* 1944), pp. 22–26.

11. Merlin P. Mitchell, "Tales of Bone Mizell, Folk Character of South Florida," *Southern Folklore Quarterly* 35 (March 1971): 34–43.

12. Ruby Elaine Whidden (comp.), "DeSoto County," manuscript, Arcadia, Florida, 1937.

13. D. B. McKay, "'Bone' Mizelle, Florida Cowboy," *Tampa* (Fla.) *Tribune,* September 12, 1948, p. 3D.

14. Wesley Stout, "Rattlesnake Johnson Took Care of Bone Mizell," *Fort Lauderdale* (Fla.) *News,* January 4, 1959, p. 6A.

15. Last will and testament of Ziba King, probated March 25, 1901, Record of Wills 1, DeSoto County, Clerk of Circuit Court Office, Arcadia, Florida, pp. 161–64.

16. J. F. Bartholf, "Pine Level, Manatee County," *Semi-Tropical* 2 (March 1876): 153–54.

17. W. D. Payne, *A Brief Sketch of the Life and Works of John W. Hendry, a Pioneer Baptist Preacher of South Florida* (Wauchula: Advocate Press, 1907), pp. 6–7.

18. Charles W. Arnade, "Cattle Raising in Spanish Florida, 1513–1763," *Agricultural History* 35 (July 1961): 116–24.

19. "Florida Spurs Its Cattle Industry," *Investor's Reader* 22 (May 5, 1954): 18–24.

20. Rupert B. Vance, *Human Geography of the South* (Chapel Hill: University of North Carolina Press, 1932), pp. 163–64.

21. Sidney Smith, "Wizard Edison in Florida," *The World* (New York City), April 3, 1887, p. 10.

22. "Florida Spurs Its Cattle Industry."

23. W. Theodore Mealor, Jr., and Merle C. Prunty, "Open-Range

Ranching in Southern Florida," *Annals of the Association of American Geographers* 66 (September 1976): 360–76.

24. Myrtle Hilliard Crow, "Cowboys Received $1 a Day—With No Soft Beds," *Osceola Sun* (Kissimmee, Fla.), July 29, 1976, p. 5.

25. Curtiss, "Punta Rassa and the Cattle Trade."

26. Frederic Remington, "Cracker Cowboys of Florida," *Harper's New Monthly Magazine* 140 (August 1895): 339–45.

27. E. W. P., "Can't Fool the Cracker," *Florida Times-Union* (Jacksonville), August 3, 1896, p. 3.

28. Crow, "Cowboys Received $1 a Day."

29. "Round-up Time Used to Be Rough-Tumble," *Arcadian* (Arcadia, Fla.), July 1, 1965, p. 5C.

30. "King of the Crackers," *New York Daily Tribune,* September 16, 1883, p. 9.

31. Crow, "Cowboys Received $1 a Day."

32. George H. Dacy, "Punta Rassa: 'Ghost Port' of Cattle Shipments to Cuba," *The Florida Cattleman* 4 (March 1940): 4–5.

33. "The South Florida Cattle Trade," *Fort Myers* (Fla.) *Press,* June 12, 1886, p. 3.

Chapter 5

Note: Chapter title from Criminal Docket 1, March 17, 1888– March 13, 1895, DeSoto County, Clerk of Circuit Court Office, Arcadia, Florida, p. 373; epigraph from "Cattle Raising in South Florida," *Florida Times-Union and Citizen* (Jacksonville), December 19, 1897, sec. 5, p. 40.

1. George H. Dacy, *Four Centuries of Florida Ranching* (St. Louis: Britt Printing Co., 1940), p. 137.

2. Ann Ryals and Sandra Welles, "Cattle, Cowboys, and Ranches," *Arcadian* (Arcadia, Fla.), June 17, 1976, pp. 2C–4C.

3. Allen H. Andrews, *A Yank Pioneer in Florida* (Jacksonville: Douglas Printing Co., 1950), pp. 309–12.

4. "The Sara Sota Thugs," *Florida Times-Union* (Jacksonville), July 23, 1885, p. 3.

5. Karl H. Grismer, *The Story of Sarasota, the History of the City and County of Sarasota, Florida* (Tampa: Florida Growers Press, 1946), pp. 79–91.

6. Francis Marion Platt, manuscript written in Central America, 1885–87, 4 pp.

7. Dora McLenon Johnston, "Additional History of the Lake Okeechobee Country," manuscript, North Fort Myers, Florida, July 1965, pp. 5–8.

8. Platt, manuscript.

9. Wesley Stout, "The Beachcomber," *Fort Lauderdale* (Fla.) *News*, October 23, 1963, p. 10A.

10. Circuit Court Minutes I, 1887–1900, DeSoto County, Clerk of Circuit Court Office, Arcadia, Florida, pp. 1, 27, 39–40, 45–46.

11. "The Platt Family Carved out Indiantown Home from Wilderness," *Stuart* (Fla.) *News*, January 9, 1964, p. 4DD.

12. A. H. Curtiss, "Punta Rassa and the Cattle Trade," *Bartow* (Fla.) *Informant*, November 24, 1883, p. 1.

13. Stetson Kennedy, *Palmetto Country* (New York: Duell, Sloan & Pearce, 1942), pp. 222–23.

14. Frederic Remington, "Cracker Cowboys of Florida," *Harper's New Monthly Magazine* 140 (August 1895): 339–45.

15. "Held as Cattle Thieves," *Florida Times-Union* (Jacksonville), July 17, 1896, p. 3.

16. "Reminiscences of Emory Leroy Lesley," manuscript, Haines City, Florida, 1864–1931, p. 17.

17. Dacy, *Four Centuries of Florida Ranching.*

18. "Cattle Raising in South Florida."

19. "Cattle Kings to Clash," *Florida Times-Union* (Jacksonville), July 19, 1895, p. 2.

20. Kennedy, *Palmetto Country.*

21. "Held as Cattle Thieves."

22. Dacy, *Four Centuries of Florida Ranching.*

23. Remington, "Cracker Cowboys of Florida."

24. "The DeSoto Cattle Case," *Courier-Informant* (Bartow, Fla.), July 8, 1896, p. 1.

25. Remington, "Cracker Cowboys of Florida."

26. "Reminiscences of Emory Leroy Lesley."

27. Remington, "Cracker Cowboys of Florida."

28. Ben Merchant Vorphal, *My Dear Wister—The Frederic Remington–Owen Wister Letters* (Palo Alto: American West Publishing Co., 1972), p. 66.

29. *Fort Myers* (Fla.) *Press*, March 29, 1888, p. 2.

30. Albert DeVane, "The Young Fellow Posed as Hub Williams, Desperado—And Met up with Real Hub!" *Tampa* (Fla.) *Tribune*, September 18, 1955, p. 20C.

31. Judge Ellis Connell May, *From Dawn to Sunset—Recollections of a Pioneer Florida Judge* (Tampa: Florida Growers Press, 1955), 2: 126–27.

32. *Sunland Tribune* (Tampa, Fla.), March 4, 1880, p. 3.

33. *Tampa* (Fla.) *Guardian*, February 28, 1880, p. 3.

34. "Quinn Bass Killed!" *Courier-Informant* (Bartow, Fla.), May 30, 1894, p. 4.

35. "Fish Eating Creek Murder," *Courier-Informant* (Bartow, Fla.), July 8, 1896, p. 1.

36. Interview with Stephen B. (Bay) Johnson, November 17, 1978, Eustis, Florida.

37. "Reminiscences of Emory Leroy Lesley."

38. "Round-up Time Used to Be Rough-Tumble," *Arcadian* (Arcadia, Fla.), July 1, 1965, p. 5C.

39. Interview with V. C. (Mose) Hollingsworth, August 9, 1978, Arcadia, Florida.

40. "To Stop Cattle Stealing," *Florida Times-Union* (Jacksonville), May 9, 1896, p. 3.

41. "Cattle Raising in South Florida."

42. Barbara Welles Probasco, letter to author, June 4, 1978.

43. Remington, "Cracker Cowboys of Florida."

44. Criminal Docket 1, March 17, 1888–March 13, 1895, DeSoto County, Clerk of Circuit Court Office, Arcadia, Florida, p. 344.

45. Bar Docket County Court 1, DeSoto County, Clerk of Circuit Court Office, Arcadia, Florida, p. 39; Minutes County Court 1, 1893–1916, p. 89; Criminal Docket 2, March 15, 1895–October 25, 1905, p. 9.

46. "Court Proceedings," *Fort Myers* (Fla.) *Press*, March 5, 1896, p. 8.

47. Circuit Court Minutes I, 1887–1900, DeSoto County, Clerk of Circuit Court Office, Arcadia, Florida, p. 427.

48. Margaret Roesch, "'Real Old-Timer' Relates Interesting Railroad Incidents," *Tampa* (Fla.) *Tribune*, December 3, 1950, p. 10C.

49. Interview with V. C. (Mose) Hollingsworth, March 23, 1978, Arcadia, Florida.

50. Circuit Court Minutes I, 1887–1900, DeSoto County, Clerk of Circuit Court Office, Arcadia, Florida, pp. 496–98.

51. Criminal Docket 3, March 9, 1906–December 9, 1916, DeSoto County, Clerk of Circuit Court Office, Arcadia, Florida, pp. 262–66; *Minutes of Circuit Court 5*, pp. 515–17.

52. Martha K. Hopkins, "'Bone' Mizell Died a Blissful Bachelor," *Tampa* (Fla.) *Tribune*, September 21, 1958, p. 8E.

53. "Fence Cutters Killed Resisted When Caught," *Polk County Record* (Bartow, Fla.), January 30, 1920, p. 1.

54. "Law and Order Will Always Prevail," *Tampa* (Fla.) *Daily Times*, January 31, 1920, p. 4.

Chapter 6

Note: Chapter title from J. Pete Schmidt, "The Painted Life of a Violent Florida Frontier," *The Floridian*, St. Petersburg (Fla.) *Times*, May 14, 1972, pp. 30–31; epigraph from Geraldine Kent Thrailkill,

"The 'Bone' Mizell Story," manuscript, Wauchula, Florida, June 1973, p. 1.

1. Marks & Brands 1, DeSoto County, Clerk of Circuit Court Office, Arcadia, Florida, p. 15.

2. "'Bones' Mizelle—DeSoto's Most Colorful Cowboy," *Arcadian* (Arcadia, Fla.), July 1, 1965, p. 1B.

3. D. B. McKay, "'Bone' Mizelle, Florida Cowboy," *Tampa* (Fla.) *Tribune*, September 12, 1948, p. 3D.

4. D. B. McKay, "Another Bone Mizelle Story," *Tampa* (Fla.) *Tribune*, February 27, 1949, p. 4D.

5. Albert DeVane, "Napoleon Bonaparte (Bone) Mizell Loved to Watch Bobcats Fighting," *Tampa* (Fla.) *Tribune*, December 28, 1958, p. 6D.

6. Merlin P. Mitchell, "Tales of Bone Mizell, Folk Character of South Florida," *Southern Folklore Quarterly* 35 (March 1971): 34–43.

7. Interview with H. Logan King, Jr., April 28, 1979, Lutz, Florida.

8. Interview with L. E. (Squash) Ford (age seventy-eight), April 9, 1979, Arcadia, Florida.

9. Ibid.

10. *Florida's DeSoto County in the Making*, edited by the 1943 freshman class of DeSoto County High School, Arcadia, Florida, 1943, pp. 2, 8.

11. "Telling of Antics of 'Bone' Mizelle," *Arcadian* (Arcadia, Fla.), April 9, 1964, p. 22B.

12. Mitchell, "Tales of Bone Mizell."

13. Ibid.

14. Interview with L. E. (Squash) Ford.

15. McKay, "'Bone' Mizelle, Florida Cowboy."

16. Mitchell, "Tales of Bone Mizell."

17. Interview with Mayo Johnston, May 23, 1978, Panama City, Florida.

18. Interview with V. C. (Mose) Hollingsworth, March 23, 1978, Arcadia, Florida.

19. Al Burt, "Here It Is Judgment Day for Bad Old Bone Mizell," *Miami* (Fla.) *Herald*, March 18, 1974, p. 10BW.

20. Ibid.

21. Mitchell, "Tales of Bone Mizell."

22. Ibid.

23. Jack Beater, *Tales of South Florida and the Ten Thousand Islands* (Fort Myers: Ace Press, 1965), pp. 110–12.

24. Stephen B. (Bay) Johnson, "Florida in the Rough," manuscript, Eustis, Florida, 1965, p. 2.

25. Mitchell, "Tales of Bone Mizell."

26. Frog Smith, "Cracker Cowboy," *Fort Myers* (Fla.) *News-Press*, July 16, 1978, pp. 1D–2D.

27. *Florida's DeSoto County in the Making.*

28. Mitchell, "Tales of Bone Mizell."

29. "Telling of Antics of 'Bone' Mizelle."

30. George Loposky, "Bone Mizell: Cracker Cowboy," *Florida Magazine, Sentinel Star* (Orlando), May 20, 1973, pp. 20, 22–23.

31. "Bevis to Be Speaker at Mizell Ceremony," *Tampa* (Fla.) *Tribune*, January 26, 1974, p. 5.

Chapter 7

Note: Chapter title from Merlin P. Mitchell, "Tales of Bone Mizell, Folk Character of South Florida," *Southern Folklore Quarterly* 35 (March 1971): 34–43; epigraph from Perry C. Hull, "A Hymn-Singing Is Legal, 'Bone' Argued, Regardless of the Singer's Condition," *Tampa* (Fla.) *Tribune*, February 8, 1959, p. 8E.

1. Rex Beach, *Wild Pastures* (New York: A. L. Burt Co., 1935), p. 16.

2. Interview with V. C. (Mose) Hollingsworth, March 23, 1978, Arcadia, Florida.

3. Interview with Mayo Johnston, May 23, 1978, Panama City, Florida.

4. D. B. McKay, "'Bone' Mizelle, Florida Cowboy," *Tampa* (Fla.) *Tribune*, September 12, 1948, p. 3D.

5. Ralph Sumner, "Bone Mizell Remembered," *Tampa* (Fla.) *Tribune*, January 13, 1963, p. 2B.

6. George W. Gatewood, *Ox Cart Days to Airplane Era in Southwest Florida* (Punta Gorda: *Punta Gorda Herald*, 1939), pp. 15–17, 22.

7. George W. Gatewood, *On Florida's Coconut Coasts* (Punta Gorda: *Punta Gorda Herald*, 1944), pp. 22–26.

8. Ibid.

9. Wesley Stout, "The Beachcomber," *Fort Lauderdale* (Fla.) *News*, January 4, 1959, p. 6A.

10. George H. Dacy, *Four Centuries of Florida Ranching* (St. Louis: Britt Printing Co., 1940), p. 156.

11. V. K. Graham, "Bone's Moan: I'm Dead and the First One Up!" *Tampa* (Fla.) *Tribune*, August 10, 1958, p. 17E.

12. Nixon Smiley, "Bone Mizelle: Will Rogers of the Cattle Rustlers," *Miami* (Fla.) *Herald*, August 20, 1967, p. 10C.

13. Wyatt Blassingame, *Live From the Devil* (Garden City, N.Y.: Doubleday & Co., 1959), pp. 86–87, 240–41.

14. Hull, "A Hymn-Singing Is Legal."

15. Smiley, "Bone Mizelle."

16. Nixon Smiley, "Blood Feud at Canoe Creek," *Sunday Magazine, Miami* (Fla.) *Herald,* April 16, 1967, pp. 8–9.

17. E. A. (Frog) Smith, "'Frog' Smith Recalls Some of Florida's Greatest Jokesters," *Tampa* (Fla.) *Tribune,* December 6, 1953, p. 14C.

18. Martha K. Hopkins, "'Bone' Mizelle Died a Blissful Bachelor," *Tampa* (Fla.) *Tribune,* September 21, 1958, p. 8E.

19. Ibid.

20. Mitchell, "Tales of Bone Mizell."

21. Interview with Mrs. Bessie Keene (age seventy-one), March 16, 1979, Holly Hill, Florida.

22. Interview with H. Logan King, Jr., April 28, 1979, Lutz, Florida.

23. Stephen Trumbull, "'Bone' Never Drew a Gun—He Joshed 'Em Dead," *Miami* (Fla.) *Herald,* January 26, 1962, pp. 1A, 24A.

24. Robert H. Morgan, letter to author, September 9, 1978.

25. Read B. Harding, "Historical Society Chooses," *Herald-Advocate* (Wauchula, Fla.), May 1, 1966, p. 1.

26. Trumbull, "'Bone' Never Drew a Gun."

27. Interview with Mrs. Bessie Keene.

28. Certificate of death, State of Florida Bureau of Vital Statistics, Jacksonville, Florida, file no. 7350, registration district no. 12-087, filed July 15, 1921.

29. "Interred at Joshua Creek," *DeSoto County News* (Arcadia, Fla.), July 22, 1921.

Chapter 8

Note: Chapter title from Frog Smith, "Wild, Wily Man of the Range," *All Florida & TV Week Magazine,* March 25, 1962, p. 5; epigraph from "Telling of Antics of 'Bone' Mizell," *Arcadian* (Arcadia, Fla.), April 9, 1964, p. 22B.

1. *Fort Myers* (Fla.) *Press,* November 9, 1893, p. 4.

2. Albert DeVane, "Napoleon Bonaparte (Bone) Mizell Loved to Watch Bobcats Fighting," *Tampa* (Fla.) *Tribune,* December 28, 1958, p. 6D.

3. Stephen Trumbull, "'Paul Bunyan' of Florida Confesses," *Miami* (Fla.) *Herald,* November 2, 1946, pp. 1A, 4A.

4. Stephen Trumbull, "'Bone' Never Drew a Gun—He Joshed 'Em Dead," *Miami* (Fla.) *Herald,* January 26, 1962, pp. 1A, 4A.

5. Kyle S. Van Landingham, "Joseph Underhill, 1795–c1881," *South Florida Pioneers* 13 (July 1977): 8–9.

6. *Marriage Bonds of Hillsborough County, Florida, 1846–1887,* compiled by Mary T. Henderson Hickman, DeSoto chapter of the Daughters of the American Revolution, 1939, bk. 1, p. 15.

7. "Soldiers of Florida," *South Florida Pioneers* 2 (October 1974): 27–28.

8. Board of State Institutions, *Soldiers of Florida in the Seminole Indian–Civil and Spanish-American Wars* (Live Oak: Democrat Book and Job Print, 1903), pp. 178–79.

9. Van Landingham, "Joseph Underhill."

10. "Early Marriage Records of Manatee County, Florida," *South Florida Pioneers* 5 (July 1975): 13; 4 (April 1975): 13.

11. 1880 Census Population Schedules, Florida (Manatee County), microcopy T9, roll 130, p. 18; National Archives and Records Service, Washington, D.C., 1885 Florida State Census Schedules (Monroe County), microcopy M845, roll 9, p. 13; 1890 Census Population Schedules, Florida (Lee County), microcopy T623, roll 172.

12. Jennie A. Reninger, "Cowhand Gives $9,000 Party," *Atlanta* (Ga.) *Journal Magazine*, March 13, 1932, p. 7.

13. *Florida's DeSoto County in the Making*, edited by the 1943 freshman class of DeSoto County High School, Arcadia, Florida, 1943, pp. 2, 8.

14. Trumbull, "'Paul Bunyan'of Florida Confesses."

15. D. B. McKay, "'Bone' Mizelle, Florida Cowboy," *Tampa* (Fla.) *Tribune*, September 12, 1948, p. 3D.

16. Ruby Leach Carson, "Ballad of Bone Mizelle," *The Florida Teacher* 4 (February–March, 1939): 14.

17. Jack Beater, *Tales of South Florida and the Ten Thousand Islands* (Fort Myers: Ace Press, 1965), pp. 110–12.

18. Wesley Stout, "The Beachcomber," *Fort Lauderdale* (Fla.) *News*, January 11, 1959, p. 6A.

19. Trumbull, "'Paul Bunyan' of Florida Confesses."

20. Nixon Smiley, "Ol' Sheiver's Bones Took a Little Trip," *Miami* (Fla.) *Herald*, March 19, 1967, p. 3F.

21. Rex Beach, *Wild Pastures* (New York: A. L. Burt Co., 1935), pp. 158–59.

22. Stout, "The Beachcomber."

23. Reninger, "Cowhand Gives $9,000 Party."

24. D. B. McKay, "Ballad Inspired by Bone Mizelle," *Tampa* (Fla.) *Tribune*, December 19, 1948, p. 3D.

25. Jabbo Gordon, "Bone Mizell—In the 1890's, He Was DeSoto's Wildest Cowboy," *Arcadian* (Arcadia, Fla.), June 17, 1976, pp. 7C–9C.

26. Interview with Frances Kay Hendry, September 20, 1978, North Fort Myers, Florida.

Chapter 9

Note: Chapter title from Ruby Leach Carson, "Ballad of Bone Mizelle," *The Florida Teacher* 4 (February–March 1939): 14; epigraph from Wesley Stout, "The Beachcomber," *Fort Lauderdale* (Fla.) *News*, February 20, 1962, p. 8A.

1. Keadward Fellany, "Looking Rearwards," *Kissimmee* (Fla.) *Valley Gazette*, special magazine edition, 1911, p. 23.

2. Minnie Moore Willson, *History of Osceola County, Florida Frontier Life* (Orlando: Inland Press, 1935), p. 13.

3. Nixon Smiley, "Ol' Sheiver's Bones Took a Little Trip," *Miami* (Fla.) *Herald*, March 19, 1967, p. 3F.

4. Dick Warner, "Bone Mizell Story Turns up Now as 'Old Bill' Yarn," *Tampa* (Fla.) *Tribune*, June 20, 1954, p. 16C.

5. Vivian Yeiser Laramore, "Singing in the Sun," *The Florida Teacher* 4 (February–March 1939): 14.

6. Charlton W. Tebeau and Ruby Leach Carson, *Florida from Indian Trail to Space Age* (Delray Beach: Southern Publishing Co., 1965), 3: 946–48.

7. Laramore, "Singing in the Sun."

8. Laramore-Rader Poetry Group, *Singing in the Sun—An Anthology of Florida Verse* (Miami Beach: Atlantic Printers and Lithographers, 1964), p. 24.

9. Geraldine Kent Thrailkill, "The 'Bone' Mizell Story," manuscript, Wauchula, Florida, June 1973, p. 1, used by permission of Geraldine Kent Thrailkill.

10. Ralph Sumner, "Memorial to Cowboy Bone Mizell Is Unveiled," *Tampa* (Fla.) *Tribune*, March 11, 1974, p. 2.

11. "'Bones' Mizelle—DeSoto's Most Colorful Cowboy," *Arcadian* (Arcadia, Fla.), July 1, 1965, p. 1B.

Index

Pine Level - Manatee County

Ft. Ogden - Depot house

Alligtor, FL now Lake City, FL.

Ft Thompson

Barbarville

Jane Green Swamp - location?